Raising Money from Trusts

RAISING MONEY FROM TRUSTS

Second edition
by Michael Norton

A Directory of Social Change Publication

RAISING MONEY FROM TRUSTS

edited and designed by Michael Norton
cover design by Ruth Lowe

Copyright © 1981, 1989 the Directory of Social Change

First published 1981. Reprinted 1984, 1987. This completely
revised second edition published 1989.

The Directory of Social Change, Radius Works, Back Lane,
London NW3 1HL. Telephone 01-435 8171

ISBN 0 907164 48 X

Typeset by Kerry Robinson at Neals Yard DTP Studio.
Printed and bound in Great Britain by Biddles of Guildford.

British Library Cataloguing in Publication Data
Raising money from trusts.
    1. Great Britain. Charities. Fund raising
    I. Norton, Michael 1942– II. Directory of Social
    Change
    361.7′0941

ISBN 0-907164-48-X

Contents

Part 1

UNDERSTANDING TRUSTS

Introduction

Overall, trusts and foundations give somewhere in the region of £500 million each year to charity, and this represents around 5 per cent of the total income of charities. It is impossible to do more than guess at these figures, because accurate, comprehensive, up-to-date information is not available. Nonetheless, trust giving is very substantial, and it is an important source of income for charitable activity.

Although there are very great differences among the many trusts that operate in the UK, as a whole they have played a very significant role in the field of charitable endeavour. Trusts fulfil their objectives by giving away money to other charities to undertake work they wish to support. It is the recipient charities who do the actual work, and the relationship between the two is that of a working partnership. Many trusts have assumed a pioneering role, funding areas of activity that are in the forefront of social change, and helping establish new ways of working and new methods of meeting social needs. This is not only a matter of 'priming the pump', of providing support for new ideas which will eventually be taken over by the statutory services, but also of finding ways of meeting the needs of society cost-effectively within the financial constraints that exist.

Trusts represent a diverse and independent sector of charitable funding. Unlike government, trusts have no statutory role. They have no responsibilities or commitments to fulfil that are not of their own choosing; and they are administered by small groups of people accountable only to themselves and limited as to what they can do by the trust deed under which the trust was established. Unlike industry, trusts are not giving away their shareholders' money, and do not have to justify their charitable giving by claiming some sort of return for it – whether some real benefit or that the company is seen as a socially responsible organisation and a good citizen in its local community.

Each trust will have its own objectives and methods of working, although in many cases these may not be very clear. Trusts have historically been very secretive, and it is only in recent years that some of them have been prepared to come out into the open and discuss how they operate. It is only for some of the large trusts that the trust's policies are actually made public.

INTRODUCTION

Often when an organisation has a fund-raising problem, an immediate response is that it should try to raise the money it needs from trusts. But it is becoming increasingly hard to raise money from trusts. Trust income has not been keeping pace with the inflation that has been occurring in the costs of the organisations they have been supporting. At the same time the demands for their money are increasing, with many more charities looking for support.

To be successful in raising money from trusts, you not only have to be doing work that will interest them, and such is the range that whatever you are doing (so long as it is charitable) you should be able to find a trust that is interested in what you are doing, but you also need to approach them in such a way that they will respond positively to your application. If you look at it from their point of view, they are all receiving a constant stream of applications – far more than they are able to support – and your application has to stand out from amongst the rest as being interesting, well thought out, and containing a well-stated case for why the trust should give you its support, if your application is to succeed.

We hope that this book will help applicants understand the world of trusts, and assist them in framing better applications to those trusts which are most likely to want to give for the sort of work they are doing.

UNDERSTANDING TRUSTS

By Ben Whitaker

I think it useful to have some understanding of the rather extraordinary creatures that charitable trusts are; and in this context I am largely referring to those bodies that give money away for charitable purposes (grant-making trusts, foundations, charitable funds), rather than those bodies that are set up to do the charitable work which may be funded by an endowment or through grants and donations or by some other means. In fact English charitable law makes no distinction between the givers and the doers, and indeed there is often no clear dividing line – many of the givers have their own programmes of work which they themselves undertake and many of the doers are themselves endowed with capital from which they derive an income.

Trusts are not simply a British phenomenon. They are most prevalent in the rich Protestant countries of the North Atlantic; they are not nearly so widespread in France and the Latin countries, perhaps because the Catholic church has in some respects assumed the role of a huge foundation. Many aspects of trusts in Britain are also applicable to trusts in other countries, and particularly in the USA, where foundations now are of great importance – some of the largest American trusts have bigger finances than some member states of the United Nations.

Trusts are a large and somewhat secretive sector of our economy that has never been adequately analysed or evaluated. Their size is not usually fully appreciated, amounting in Britain to well over £6 billion of assets and £0.5 billion of income each year. They are extremely diverse in their natures, reflecting the motivations of their founders which are equally diverse. Looking at their historical roots gives a fascinating insight into British life over the centuries. For example one trust, the Week's Charity, was founded to purchase faggots to burn heretics (advancement of religion) whilst another was started in order to deport foreign bullfighters (other purposes beneficial to the community). These are two rather extreme examples, but the motivation of those who endow trusts, just like the motivation of those who work in the charitable field, is complex.

The most famous foundation in the USA, the Ford Foundation, was started rather unphilanthropically as an attempt to keep the control of the motor company within the family; but out of that has emerged the best known, liberal, international foundation in the world. Similarly, Rockefeller started his foundation mostly to annoy his family – the original John D Rockefeller disliked human nature. It is one of the ironies of history that out of mean-minded fanatical misers such as these have flowed some very beneficial results.

What a trust can do is outlined in its objects clause contained in its trust deed. These objects are formulated when the trust is established, in many cases in very specific terms. Thus a lot of trusts are still determined from the past. A radical Charity Commissioner called Arthur Hobhouse in the nineteenth century railed against what he called 'government from the grave'. He thought it totally wrong that a man who has made his money was able to control it after he was dead by tying it up in a trust and specifying how the income should be spent. He believed that money ought to be circulating in society according to contemporary needs and contemporary relevance. But a rich man with a skilled lawyer can set up a trust for old Etonians (or for that matter old goats) and ensure that the trust will do this in perpetuity, regardless of the state of British education or the goat population.

It is possible, but difficult, to change the objects of a trust. Under the legal doctrine of 'Cy Pres', the trustees can say that what they intend to do is the nearest equivalent today of the founder's original intentions, when the original objects are obsolete. Smith's Charity which owns housing in West London was founded 'for the relief and ransom of poor captives being slaves under the Turkish pirates' and now has an income of several million pounds a year; over the years there has been a great deal of discussion as to how these objects could be interpreted in the modern world. It is just possible that these objects would cover the freeing of hostages in Lebanon (which was once part of the Ottoman Empire). But fortunately this trust had other objects which are still capable of being fulfilled (including the relief of the poor in a wide range of parishes, the support of poor

4

clergy and the relief of 'my poor kindred'), and it is here that the trust is believed now to concentrate its grant-making. To change the actual objects of a trust (apart from very small trusts) requires a private bill through Parliament, which is both a cumbersome and an expensive procedure. Occasionally a number of obsolete trusts have been amalgamated and re-formed – the City Parochial and Cripplegate Foundations are two such, combining a myriad of local charities in London (City Parochial) and in the Southern part of Islington bordering the City (Cripplegate). The Charity Commission is eager to promote other such modernisations, and the 1985 Charities Act simplified the procedure for local charities for the relief of the poor.

If you feel that a trust has become out-of-date or irrelevant, it is actually quite difficult to apply any pressure. The trustees may feel that this is implied criticism and so clam up; trustees are normally responsible for electing new trustees, so it is unlikely that you would be offered a trusteeship and a chance to participate in their discussions and reform the trust from within. An intelligent article in the local newspaper and argument from precedent (many trustees are lawyers and would respond to this line) are probably the best hopes.

One aspect of the problem is where the trust's objects have become out-of-date. A second aspect is the whole concept of what is charitable and what is not. What a trust can do or give money to and what it cannot, is based on the two main charity laws which date from 1601 and 1891. These charity laws define four main categories or 'heads' of charitable activity – relief of poverty; advancement of religion; advancement of education; and other purposes beneficial to the community. There are many anomalies. One surprise is that almost anything connected with animals is deemed charitable, whereas what can be done to further the welfare of the human animal is much more restricted. The Charity Commission has the job of deciding what is charitable and what is not within the 1891 framework and based on precedents set by decided court cases. Whereas there is some scope for flexibility, many modern needs of society could not have been foreseen at the time the law was drafted. In an ideal world almost any project which was of benefit to mankind, to the public or to the community at large should be counted as charitable and have tax-exempt status; this is, in effect, the proposal of the Charity Law Reform Group. There have been sporadic attempts to interpret charity law in a more modern and

5

relevant way. The most recent attempt to reform charity law was the Goodman Committee, but even its very limited suggestions for reform were not implemented. The charity lobby is immensely strong, particularly in the House of Lords, and any government knows that any attempt to introduce change will arouse enormous passions. The White Paper on charity reform published in 1989 and the Charities Act which will follow it avoid the issue of a definition altogether, and concentrate on the reform of administrative procedures for the regulation of charities. So there is a reluctance to do anything, and we seem stuck with the status quo which will continue for better or worse.

The whole range of human nature is present in the interests which trusts seek to address. Each trust is different and has its own concerns and approach to grant-making. Some of the motivations are extremely easy to fathom. Someone whose children have been victims of spina bifida may want to endow a research fund for that purpose. Other people, perhaps, have made a great deal of money, and perhaps they have done this somewhat unscrupulously and their trust might be described as a 'passport to heaven' or a 'fire-escape from Hades'. Other trusts exist perhaps to advertise the name of the donor; some people like putting up buildings named after them or with a plaque saying that it was donated by XYZ. The buildings of Harvard University alone include the Widener Library, Houghton Library, Lock Theatre, Harkness Commons, Kresge Hall, Lamont Library, Lehmann Hall, Mellon Hall, Morgan Hall and Strauss Hall. At some other colleges even the bathroom fittings are alleged to be named in memory of someone! At the other extreme there are very modest people who crave anonymity. One well-known British Trust, the Marble Arch Trust which was founded by the C & A Stores family, always insists on remaining anonymous; it is now referred to as 'the anonymous trust'; and when recipients state that they have received a grant from an anonymous trust, this is often an indication of the source! The larger 29th May 1961 Charitable Trust which gives some preference to charities in Coventry and Warwickshire is another trust which insists on anonymity. Whatever the motivation, I do think that charitable money should be used in the best possible way for the needs of society today. This is the challenge that trustees, who are responsible for grant decisions, should seek to address.

In fact, it can be extremely difficult to find out how most trusts do spend their money. The Inland Revenue is concerned that their tax exempt status is not abused, but any dealings between the Revenue and any particular trust are confidential. The Charity Commission is concerned that the trustees do not stray outside the charitable objects as set out in the trust deed. Some degree of public accountability is required in this partnership between private money (trust income) and public money (tax relief). The extent of this tax relief enjoyed by trusts now exceeds well over £100 million each year. All trusts with a permanent endowment are required to lodge their annual accounts with the Charity Commission, although some are very tardy in doing this. Some submit reports and many provide lists of donations that they have made, and these are open for public inspection. Some of the larger trusts publish regular reports which set out their policies. Some of the more liberal ones are reported in the press from time to time because they do interesting and occasionally controversial work. But a lot of money is locked away in near-total secrecy, although it is probably put to honest ends.

I believe that there should be greater public accountability. The minimum that trusts should be asked to do in return for the benefits they enjoy is to submit not only their annual accounts, but also an annual report of their work and a statement of their objectives, so that at least the nature of their activity could be examined. The 1989 White Paper seeks to address this by providing firmer guidelines on what information has to be lodged at the Charity Commission and at what intervals, and by putting pressure on trustees to fulfil their responsibilities.

Only if there is a wide range of applicants, presumably, is a trust able to make the most effective use of its resources by selecting the most deserving causes. Many trusts exist only to fulfil the charitable activities of the founder and do not respond to unsolicited appeals. Even though they may not respond, these 'private' trusts should be open to application and perhaps, as a result, to influence. Publicly available information on trusts through the Charity Commission Register and as digested by the various grant guides that are now available, together with a flow of applications from grant-seekers, is one way of promoting public accountability of trusts. Another idea is that of a public trustee, which was suggested by some members of the Goodman Committee as a means of seeing that the trust pursued its objectives with honesty and reasonable energy. The City Parochial Foundation, which is a major trust operating in the Greater London area spending £2 million a year in grants, has five public trustees. But this is the exception rather than the rule.

The character of a trust is principally shaped by the legal document setting it up. In many cases this is highly restrictive, with narrow objects and a small geographical area in which the trust can make grants. But whether the trust is constrained by its objects or by the wishes of its founder, the money will only be available for the purposes for which the trust was founded. Those who found trusts are not a representative group in society, and obviously their own concerns predominate. This means that money may be tied up in animal welfare, public school education or the maintenance of regimental silver, rather than available to meet the most pressing needs of society today.

The second limiting factor is the trustees, who are responsible for interpreting the founder's wishes and deciding on how the trust money should be spent. Trustees are not a representative group. I estimate them to be 95% male and 99.9% white. The vast majority are middle-class and mostly of 'a certain age'. Trustees are a self-perpetuating group; for most trusts, the existing trustees have the responsibility of electing any new trustees. Even the best intentioned may not know people from a different social background whom they would entrust with the task of working together as co-trustees. The characteristics of trusts, that they are white, male, middle-class and middle-aged, certainly affects their outlook. It may explain the dearth of funding for programmes which particularly help women, or ethnic minorities, or which arise from an understanding of the problems which face working-class people – this is not to say that a lot of trustees are not genuinely concerned to help the 'deserving poor', but that they have an inevitable lack of comprehension about what working-class life is like. Similarly, in race relations the white view would predominate at the expense of self-determined solutions.

The third limiting factor is geography. The majority of trusts are centred in London and the South East. It is harder for them to work away from their own area since the trustees mostly see the problems and meet people from that area. The social needs of Belfast, Glasgow, Merseyside and Tyneside (not to mention those faced by people living in rural areas) are just as great, if not greater than those of Notting Hill or Brixton which happen to be close to home. I remember after the race riots in Notting Hill in the 1960s that it was impossible to walk through the area without bumping into a researcher or a community worker; trustees would do well to remember that there are urgent and pressing problems in other parts of Britain. Some trusts are beginning to address this problem. The Royal Jubilee Trusts, including the Prince's Trust, have a network of local grant committees covering the country. The Baring Foundation has advisers in the North East (including Cleveland) and the North West, where it makes special allocations. A number of other trusts are beginning to make a conscious effort to shift the emphasis of their grant-making away from the South East.

The fourth limiting factor is the applications that a trust receives. Some may not consider applications, while others actively seek them out. There will always be a lot of general mailings and general appeals, but most of the serious applications will be determined by what people think the trust will give to. This will be determined by any statements of policy and also from past experience. But just because a trust has a reputation for something in the past, it does not mean that this will continue; a change of mind of one of the trustees, or the appointment of a new trustee or director, or even the eloquence and urgency of the application may be able to influence its policies and change its future direction. At present there is no mechanism for trusts to communicate their interests to intending applicants or to suggest areas of activity that they might be interested in apart from the published grant guides, which are published at two-yearly intervals. But this is something that might emerge as the trust world continues to develop – although many trustees still see grant-seekers as an intrusion into their private and rather cosy world of giving money away.

The fifth limiting factor arises from charity law. Trustees may only spend money to further their charitable objects; however the law limits this still further by restricting them from 'political activity'. This is a simple bargain – in return for the tax-exempt status and all the benefits that flow from that, the charity may not involve itself in politics. Some trusts (a very few) have decided to pay tax and be non-charitable so that they are not constrained in this respect; the best known is the Joseph Rowntree Social Service Trust which amongst other things has had a long tradition of supporting the former Liberal Party. Politics is a controversial area, and it is also something of a grey area where hard and fast definitions of what is political and what is not are impossible. There are in the annual reports of the Charity Commissioners squeaks and rumblings about what they consider to be areas of concern along this difficult borderline.

It is quite obvious that charitable money should not be used for Party Politics, but there is a very strong cost-effective argument that charities should not continually spend their money pouring wine into a leaking bottle. Besides bandaging the wounds, trusts should try to delve a little deeper and find out something about the causes of the problem and do something about these. The contrast between doing the first aid work and seeking the necessary structural changes is seen in the way famine relief charities have moved into development and public education work. And there is even a point of view that by palliating present problems we put off structural change, thereby in the longer term doing more harm than good. Tackling the causes might well involve lobbying and putting pressure on government to change the law or to take over responsibility for a particular problem. This is something that may arise more and more in the future as funds become increasingly limited.

The practice of charities keeping out of politics certainly benefits the status quo. For example, the Lord's Day Observance Society had charitable status in order to carry out its work of preserving the Sunday trading laws; but an organisation setting itself up to change the Sunday laws would be deemed political and refused charitable status. If charities are prevented from seeking changes in the law, their action is inevitably biased towards supporting the status quo. Charities are allowed to educate and inform, and they are allowed to further their objects in all manner of ways through powers conferred in their founding documents, and so to some extent political activity is permitted. Indeed, government often seeks the views of charities on issues in which they have a special interest, but can get very angry when it is the charity that is taking the initiative and putting forward a partisan (opposing) viewpoint too effectively. What is political (and acceptable) and what is POLITICAL (and not) is not clear. Many trusts and charities steer clear of this contentious area. They do not want the publicity, and they do not want the bother of any confrontation with the Charity Commission or Inland Revenue. The role of trusts in funding more (non-party) political work and in becoming less concerned with first-aid work is certainly something that many trustees should be considering carefully.

Trusts have several very important roles to play arising from their independence. They are not the government and cannot hope to take over the role of government. This provides them with the opportunity, some would say the responsibility, of pioneering the way for government, of filling in the gaps between the statutory programmes, and of doing the unpopular work which a government – always with an eye on the next election – finds it difficult to do. Trusts should also bear in mind those causes that have little popular appeal; where they see great need but little support from the public, there is certainly an opportunity for them to use their money creatively. I would like to see many more trusts working in this creative way. Although some, and particularly a few of the larger ones, are liberal in their approach and are working at the frontiers of society, the vast majority miss this opportunity and are ultra-conservative in what they support.

One role that trusts have seen as theirs is that of 'pump-priming', of providing the starter money to get a project going until the idea has diffused into society or someone else has been found to take over responsibility for the funding. In part, this arises from their wish to innovate, but also from their fear of tying up their funds for a long period. It often means that an arbitrary period is set of one year or three years which relates more to the trust's funding criteria than to the needs of the project – and applicant organisations are equally good at playing this game, if it will help them get the money. The danger is that a good project will be got going and then left in mid-air if nobody is prepared to fund it. Some trusts which used to pump-prime are reconsidering their policies now that money is less readily available from other sources, as they are much more worried about the possibility of becoming locked into a project or programme for a long period. Some are resigned to the fact that they will have to provide support over a more extended period and are prepared to fund selected projects for five years or even more.

Another role that trusts can begin to play is to suggest structural change in the charities they wish to support. A great growth in voluntary organisations occurred during the 1970s when public finance became available on an increasing scale, and more organisations began to employ professional staff. During the 1980s, the system began to crack, with public finance coming under pressure, and trusts being unable to respond adequately to the increasing demand for their resources. In the 1990s, voluntary organisations will need to move away from the concept of grant aid as the sole or even main source of support, and begin to develop their own income through fund-raising, through selling their services, and by developing new relationships as partners, agents or contractors with their local authorities. All this will require skills and resources that the organisations may not now have, and it is here that trusts have an opportunity to deploy their resources, investing in the longer-term success of organisations, rather than tackling the immediate social problems of the day.

Most trusts invest their capital in stocks and shares and in property and then apply the income for charitable purposes. Those that are 'permanently endowed' can only spend income and cannot distribute their capital. But many trusts are not permanently endowed. These are free to spend their capital, but if they do this, the result will be that their investment income will decline year by year. The Ford Foundation in the USA has a policy of spending capital because they think it wrong that they should sit on their money whilst social problems are so urgent.

One of the duties of the trustees is to ensure that the capital is well invested. One idea which has taken root in the USA and which some trusts in this country are pursuing is that the capital can be invested to further their objects. For the Dartington Trust this means investing in small businesses in Devon to further their aims of rural regeneration; for a Catholic housing group it might mean preferentially lodging their money with a Catholic building society (for both Catholic and housing reasons), and for many it might mean avoiding 'socially irresponsible' companies. However, the caveat is that the money must be soundly invested, otherwise the trustees will be derelict in their duty. This puts a certain limitation on what can be done in this respect.

One problem that trusts face is that they often have very little to go on other than a written application. Many of the larger trusts now employ at least a Secretary or Director who can get out and visit some of the applicant projects, and sometimes the trustees will do this too. Some employ a panel of specialist advisers to whom they refer applications for comment. But in most cases it is the written application that is important. One danger is that a lot of people who do very worthwhile work have a talent for organising but are not quite so good at writing a honeyed letter to a trust; whereas those who are brilliant at the letter and have the ability to seize on a good idea and tune in to the special foundation language may not be quite so good at putting their ideas into practice. So trustees really should read between the lines. A badly written appeal may not always

12

signify a badly organised project, and conversely those who produce brilliant, glossy appeal literature may in fact be spending all their time doing that and nothing else.

Those who are applicants should try to put themselves in the place of the trustees when they meet to consider their giving, who are having to reject many more applications than they can possibly fund, who are feeling vaguely worried and guilty, who are troubled about the state of the economy and the country, the state of society or perhaps the breakdown of the family, and who are not at all sure what they can do about all this. The applicant may not be able to provide all the answers, but has to communicate the importance and urgency of her or his work. Trust funding is a partnership between those who have the money and those who can persuade them to part with it, and both parties are seeking similar objectives, one through giving the other by doing.

Ben Whitaker is the author of 'The Foundations', the former Director of the Minority Rights Group and now the UK Director of the Gulbenkian Foundation, a major Portuguese foundation with a UK and Ireland grants programme run from the UK.

FACTS AND FIGURES ABOUT TRUSTS

The trust sector is important to grant-seeking charities for two reasons: firstly, a substantial sum of money is given in grants each year and, secondly, the income of trusts *has to be* applied for charitable purposes (unlike the other main charitable sources such as government, companies, individuals who can all vary their level of giving, or even decide not to give at all). For this reason, getting support from trusts should be an important part of the fund-raising activity of most grant-seekers.

The relative importance of trust in the grant-making spectrum is shown in the following table:

Statutory sources

Central government support (1986/87)	£184 million
Urban Programme support (1986/87)	£ 95 million
Government training for the unemployed (1986/87)	£613 million
Housing Corporation (1988/89)	£737 million
Arts Council (1988/89)	£150 million
Local government (1986/87)	£402 million
Tax reliefs on investments and covenant income(1986/87)	
	£600 million
Rate reliefs (1986/87)	£145 million

Company support

Cash donations (1987)	£135 million
Other community contributions (1987 estimate)	£115 million

Public giving

Legacies (1987)	£400 million
Media appeals and telethon (1988)	£120 million

Grant-making trusts

Grants to charitable organisations	£400 million
Grants to individuals	£100 million

The Top Trusts

The top 25 trusts listed in the 1989 edition of the *Guide to the Major Trusts* were:

Rank	Grants	Trust	Main grant area
1	£38,500,000	Wellcome Trust	Medical and veterinary research, history of medicine
2	£25,000,000	Telethon trusts	General charitable purposes
3	£13,916,000	BBC Children in Need Appeal	Child Welfare
4	£11,000,000	Royal Society	Promotion of the natural sciences
5	£9,217,000	Tudor Trust	Social welfare, health, education
6	£7,500,000	Sainsbury Family Charitable Trusts	General charitable purposes
7	£7,200,000	Wolfson Foundation	Medicine/health, science/technology, arts/humanities
8	£6,000,000	Leverhulme Trust	Research, education
9	£5,500,000	Henry Smith's Charity	Health, social welfare, medical research
10	£5,098,000	Garfield Weston Foundation	Medicine, social welfare, arts
11	£4,310,000	Rank Foundation	Christian causes, medicine, youth, education, general
12	£4,058,000	Edith & Isaac Wolfson Charitable Trust	Jewish charities, medical and other charitable purposes
13	£3,500,000	Nuffield Foundation	Science and medicine, social research and experiment, education, care of old people, research in ageing, fellowships and awards for the Commonwealth, research into rheumatism
14	£2,897,000	Heart of Variety	Children, 'Sunshine' coaches/mini buses
15	£2,882,000	Moorgate Trust Fund + the New Moorgate Trust Fund	Medicine, disabled, arts, environment
16	£2,677,000	Bernard Sunley Foundation	General charitable purposes

15

17	£2,600,000	Baring Foundation	Social welfare, medicine, the arts, education, conservation
18	£2,500,000	Marble Arch Group of Trusts	Religion, education, social welfare, medicine
19	£2,500,000	Church Urban Fund	Social welfare and Christian development in disadvantaged urban areas
20	£2,500,000	Thames Help Trust	Welfare of children and young people in the Thames TV area
21	£2,366,000	J W Laing Trust	Christian evangelism; other charitable purposes
22	£2,312,000	Philip and Pauline Harris Charitable Settlement	Medicine, general
23	£2,107,000	Joseph Rowntree Memorial Trust	Social research and development
24	£2,032,000	Esmee Fairbairn Charitable Trust	Economic education, general charitable causes
25	£2,000,000	Charity Projects	Young people suffering from homelessness, from alcohol or drug abuse or from disability

This list is interesting in its diversity. It contains major companies which are wholly or substantially owned by charitable trusts: Wellcome, Wimpey (Tudor Trust), Baring's Bank, M&G (Esmee Fairbairn). It contains old and new philanthropy: Wolfson, Sainsbury, Nuffield, Rowntree. It contains a number of fund-raising charities which have recently emerged as amongst the largest grant-makers in the country through the exploitation of telethon fund-raising techniques: Telethon trusts (ITV), BBC Children in Need, Charity Projects. It contains other trusts which have to raise money first before they can give it away: Heart of Variety, Church Urban Fund. Together these 25 trusts distribute £140 million in grants each year.

Activities Supported

In general, trusts are able to support the whole range of charitable activity (within each trust's permitted objects). In practice, what most trusts support reflects their own particular interests and

FACTS AND FIGURES

concerns. The 1989 edition of the *Guide to the Major Trusts* analysed the giving of the top 400 trusts which together spend £286 million on grants each year.

The figures are as follows:

Health and Welfare		**£114 million**	**40%**
General welfare	£63 million (22%)		
Children	£25 million (9%)		
Youth	£10 million (4%)		
Health/disability	£16 million (6%)		
Research		**£82 million**	**29%**
Medical	£57 million (20%)		
Scientific	£15 million (6%)		
Other	£9 million (3%)		
Education		**£20 million**	**9%**
Art and Environment		**£14 million**	**4%**
Arts	£6 million (2%)		
Buildings	£4 million (1%)		
Environment	£4 million (1%)		
Religion		**£26 million**	**9%**
Christian	£14 million (5%)		
Jewish	£12 million (4%)		
Local welfare		**£16 million**	**6%**
Overseas		**£3 million**	**1%**
Other		**£11 million**	**4%**
Total trust expenditure (400 trusts)		**£286 million**	**100%**

There are inevitably distortions arising from the existence of large trusts with special interests. For example, the Wellcome Trust contributed £38 million of the £57 million for Medical Research; the medical fund-raising charities, which have not been included in this analysis, added a further £100 million. The Scientific Research category is dominated by £11 million from the Royal Society; the Other Research category includes the £6 million from Leverhulme.

Geography

Most trust money is administered from London and the South East. This does not mean that it is all spent in London and the South East; but many trusts do view the world from the perspective of where they are located, and it is far easier to build contacts and relationships with people close to you rather than in the outer extremities of the country.

Some trusts are making an attempt to counter the South East bias, and are working on the principle that they should spend at least a part of their funds in areas of greatest need (which are often those areas where little trust money is located). The Baring Foundation, for example, has appointed advisers for the North West and for the North East and Cleveland and is also working with a number of other foundations to bring more trust money into these regions.

For the first edition of this book (published in 1981) we included an analysis of trust income by region, which showed the following:

Region	Income of trusts based in the region as a proportion of the total	Population	Relative trust income per head (South East =100)
South East	91.3%	33.9m	100
East Anglia	0.7%	2.0m	15
South West	1.6%	4.4m	13
North East/North	1.1%	3.1m	13
Wales	0.9%	2.8m	12
Yorkshire/ Humberside	1.5%	4.8m	12
West Midlands	1.5%	5.2m	11
North West	1.4%	6.5m	8

Thus for every one pound of disposable trust income per head of population administered locally in the South East, each person in the North West had 8 pence. This is before taking into account the relative needs of the area and not allowing for the fact that trusts may be spending some (or even all) of their income outside the region where they are based.

These figures do demonstrate an extremely strong South East bias. What it means is that applicants from other regions need to work harder in building up their contacts; they need to stress the importance and urgency of need in their area, based if possible on statistics; and they might also wish to stress the lack of alternative sources of funds in their area. Above all, though, they need to sit down and apply to trusts. If they don't, they won't stand a chance of getting any support.

Types of Trust

Trusts come in all shapes and sizes, founded for different reasons and at different times. It is the diversity of the trust world that is one of its prominent features, and its strength. Each trust sets about the work of giving away money in its own unique way, and this means that most grant-seekers will be able to identify at least some trusts which share their interests and attitudes and which may be prepared to support their work.

The main types of trust are described below.

1. Charitable status

Charitable trusts: almost all trusts are established for charitable purposes which means that they can only make grants to charitable organisations or for charitable purposes.

Non-Charitable trusts: these are trusts which are able to make grants for both charitable and non-charitable purposes. The two best-known in the voluntary sector are the Barrow Cadbury Fund and the Joseph Rowntree Social Service Trust, both of which are associated with charitable trusts.

2. Geography

Local trusts: trusts with a limited geographical area of benefit or which have a policy of giving some or all of their money locally. For example, the Cripplegate Foundation is an amalgamation of various local charities and can only make grants in two parishes on the fringes of the City of London. The 29th May 1961 Charity is a large charity with a national beneficial area, but which gives some priority to appeals from Coventry and the West Midlands.

Community trusts: a newer brand of trust which seeks to raise capital and income from the local community in order to be able to support local projects. The Tyne and Wear Foundation and the Greater Bristol Trust are examples of these new community trusts. The Watford Flower Fund has been going somewhat longer and raises its money through donations in lieu of flowers at local funerals.

Regional trusts: a few trusts have a region as their area of support. The various trusts associated with the ITV Telethon 88 give money exclusively within their TV franchise regions. The Northern Ireland Voluntary Trust has been established to support projects in Northern Ireland.

National trusts: most trusts have a national remit, but some may concentrate their giving within certain preferred areas often including the area where they operate from. For example, the Wates Foundation gives some priority for local projects in South London.

3. Objects and policies

Specialist trusts: some trusts support very specific types of work only. This gives them a certain expertise in their grant-making. The Urban Trust supports economic regeneration projects in inner city areas having special regard to the needs of black and ethnic minority communities. The Metropolitan Drinking Fountains and Cattle Troughs Association provides grants for drinking fountains in London. The Wellcome Trust, which is the largest UK trust, supports medical research and the history of medicine.

General trusts: most trusts make grants over a wide range of activities although they may have formal or informal policies or certain excluded categories which limit the scope of their grant-making. The Tudor Trust is the largest general purpose trust spending over £9 million annually on child welfare, youth, handicap, disability, the elderly, housing, homelessness, community welfare, employment creation, training, welfare of the unemployed, conservation, the environment, the arts and education.

Relief in need trusts: many older trusts were set up to provide relief to those in need – the poor or the elderly or others in necessitous circumstances. For example, Sir Titus Salt's Charity makes a single £2 grant each year to people over 75 in Shipley, Basildon and Windhill in West Yorkshire. Fred Towler's charity makes one-off grants for holidays and necessities for residents of at least two years standing in the Diocese of Bradford. There are also many Occupational Charities (including Services Charities), whose grant-making is tied to people who have worked in particular trades or professions. There are company welfare charities, which are tied to companies and available for relief-in-need grants to former employees and their dependants.

Educational trusts: as with relief in need, there are many trusts established to make grants to individuals for educational purposes. These divide into those providing scholarships or bursaries for academic excellence, and those providing necessities such as books, clothing, support for educational visits and school journeys, whose support is based on individual financial need.

4. Links

Families of trusts: some trusts are part of a group which operate in collaboration or occasionally as one trust. The Chase, Lankelly and Hambland Trusts all have the same administration. The Sainsbury Family Trusts which include the Gatsby Charitable Foundation, the Monument Trust, the Linbury Trust, the Headley Trust, the Elizabeth Clark Charitable Trust and the Kay Kendall Leukaemia Fund, operate together and in close contact with the giving of J Sainsbury plc. The point here is that multiple or circular applications will show up, unless care is taken in sorting out the mailing beforehand.

Company trusts: many trusts are linked to companies in some way. Some like the De La Rue Jubilee Trust, the Allied Lyons Charitable Trust and the Julian Melchett Trust (British Steel) are simply vehicles for the company's giving and should be approached for funds on the basis that they are a company rather than a trust.

Some may over time have become largely independent of the company to which they were once attached, and some may continue to have close links. A few companies are wholly or substantially owned by charitable trusts (Baring's Bank, Heron Corporation, Wellcome Foundation, George Wimpey, M & G Unit Trusts and John Laing are some examples).

Private trusts: many trusts, particularly many of the very small trusts, have been set up for the tax-effective giving of an individual or a family, and are really only interested in supporting charities known to the trustees. For example, GP Charitable Trust prefers to give medium-term support for a number of charities already known to the trustees, and the Gazoni Charitable Trust has its funds fully committed for local projects and objects which are personally known to the trustees. These trusts are not private, in the sense that the money is available for public benefit, but they are private in the sense that only causes with a personal link to the founder or the trustees will normally stand any chance of getting support.

Livery companies: the City Livery Companies all have charitable trusts which they administer. Some are well known and substantial (Skinners, Mercers, Goldsmiths), others less so. Often the funds are applied for purposes connected with the livery company or the trade it represents. For example, the Saddlers Company Charitable Fund has as its objects the support of the City of London, the saddlery trade, the equestrian world, education and general charities. Alongside these funds there may be other funds bequeathed by liverymen to be administered by the Livery Company. Similar but really a separate category, are the Masonic charities including the Grand Charity.

Independent trusts: many trusts do not have any particular links or ties. They operate under the control of trustees for public benefit within their terms of the Trust Deed. Obviously, the particular interests of the trustees will play some importance in determining what is supported and what is not, and any personal contact with the trustees will never be unhelpful.

5. Where the money has come from

Trusts funded by capital transfer or endowment: this is the normal route to setting up a trust. Someone who has made a pile, decides to give some or all of it to a charitable trust. Recent examples are Paul Hamlyn who sold his Octopus publishing empire and put £50 million of the proceeds into the Paul Hamlyn Foundations or Gerald Ronson who put half the shares of his privately-owned company Heron International into the Ronson Foundation, or the J Paul Getty Jnr Charitable Trust which was established by Paul Getty. Obviously the same thing happens on a more modest scale as well.

Trusts funded by a legacy or a will: some people decide to establish a foundation on their death, bequeathing all or a part of their wealth for that purpose. Arthur Koestler's will established a foundation which has funded a chair in Parapsychology at Oxford. Some wills provide for a distribution of funds to charities selected by the executive. Although this does not create a permanent trust fund it does provide a pool of income from which grants can be made. Smee & Ford, a firm of legal agents, provides a service informing charities when such bequests are made, so that they can then apply to the executors for a grant.

Trusts funded by public subscription: the Queen's Silver Jubilee Trust, the Winston Churchill Memorial Fund, and the South Atlantic Fund are all examples of trusts funded by public subscription – often to commemorate an event, a death or in response to a natural or national disaster.

Trusts funded by mass media fund-raising: telethons, radiothons and other media appeals are a recent phenomenon. In 1988, over £100 million was raised in this way. BBC Children in Need Trust, Capital Radio Help a London Child Trust and Charity Projects (funded partly by Comic Relief) are examples.

Trusts funded by fund-raising events: some trusts organise fund-raising events as a means of obtaining the funds they need. The Prince's Trust and the Heart of Variety (which is associated with the Variety Club of Great Britain) are examples.

Trusts funded by other trusts: intermediary trusts seeking money from trusts and other sources to donate onwards using their particular expertise in grant-making are more common in the US than in the UK. However, examples do exist here – the Urban Trust, the Northern Ireland Voluntary Trust and some community trusts, for example.

Trusts funded by trading activities: a very few trusts acquire funds for distribution by entering into some form of trading activity. The Helping Hand Gift Shops produce an income which goes to support several grant-making trusts, including the Phyllis Trust.

FACTS AND FIGURES

The Wallington Missionary Marts and Auction sells second-hand furniture and jewellery from an 8,000 sq ft warehouse to support Christian missionary work.

Trusts funded by a charity reconstruction: occasionally a charity will cease providing a charitable service, sell up its assets and invest the proceeds to provide an income for distribution. The Finnart House Trust once operated a community home for the benefit of Jewish children, but now makes grants for Jewish children in need from a £3 million fund realised from the sale of its residential premises in Surrey. The 1989 Charity Commission Report highlighted a local charity, the Hampton Fuel Allotment Charity, which realised over £20 million from the sale of land to Sainsbury's for a superstore, whose purposes are being widened and will become a major local charity which will include grant-making amongst its functions.

Trusts funded by a company reconstruction: often at the time when a company goes public, it is decided to establish a charitable foundation as a part of the reconstruction of the company. The Laura Ashley Foundation and the four TSB Foundations (in England and Wales, Scotland, Northern Ireland and the Channel Islands) are examples. Occasionally a company will decide to endow a charitable trust in order to create a capital fund from which to make charitable distributions. The Nationwide Centenary Fund and the Yorkshire Bank Charitable Trust are examples.

Trusts funded by individuals out of income: some individual donors establish charitable trusts as a vehicle for their tax-effective giving. They contribute a regular annual amount to the trust under a Deed of Covenant for distribution to the charities they wish to support (a half-way house trust), or they use their annual contributions to build up a capital fund which is invested to produce an income for distribution to charity (an accumulation trust).

Trusts funded by company staff out of earned income: some companies now encourage philanthropy amongst their staff, either by covenant giving, or by payroll deduction, or by general fund-raising, with the funds contributed or raised being put into a trust under the control of staff representatives. The Allied Dunbar Staff Charity Fund and the Allied Dunbar Foundation are examples. These are likely to support projects of interest to and selected by the staff.

6. Size

Trusts vary in size from upwards of a billion pounds of assets to very little indeed. The size of the trust will influence how it is administered, the scale of its grant-making and the type of grants it makes.

What Trusts Fund

1.Types of support

Like trusts themselves, trust funding serves a variety of purposes:

An outright grant of money which would only be repayable if it could not be spent in accordance with the purposes for which it was given or any conditions made by the donor when making the gift. Grants come in the following forms:

Single payments or one-off grants.

Term grants' longer term support for a stated period of years (for most trusts, this is likely to be no more than 3 years although a few are moving towards 5-year grants).

Annual subscription payments where the same charities are supported each year.

A conditional grant, made conditional on other funds being secured or financial targets achieved.

A challenge grant for a part of the total required, challenging other funders to provide matching funds.

An underwriting, where money is pledged conditional on it not being raised from another source.

A loan, which may be either interest-bearing or interest-free.

A loan guarantee where the trust does not actually put up any money, but provides a guarantee of repayment for the lender who does.

The provision of services or premises is rare in the trust world, but the Joseph Rowntree Social Service Trust does provide premises to certain campaigning organisations, and other trusts have provided facilities for charities with which they are closely connected.

2. Purposes of the grant

Grants may be made for the following purposes:

A **contribution** towards the general costs, the core costs or the administrative costs of the organisation.

Support for a **project,** which is a specific item of work or activity being undertaken by the organisation.

A contribution towards the purchase or development of **premises.**

The purchase of a piece of **equipment** or a specific item of expenditure.

Support for **innovation** where the outcome of the project may be of some national significance. Innovation includes new ways of tackling old problems as well as dealing with new problems.

Support for **research.**

Support for an **evaluation.**

Support for **structural changes** in the organisation to allow it to proceed from one phase in its development to another. This is in a sense an 'investment' in the future of the organisation.

Other forms of **investment** such as the installation of a computer to underpin a membership drive or covenant campaign, or the production of a video or a well-designed annual report to help the organisation market its services more effectively.

Glossary of Trust Terms

The following are some of the words commonly used in connection with trusts, and an explanation of what they actually mean.

Acknowledgement of support
Most trusts require no high profile publicity or acknowledgement for the support they have given, although for some this can be important (eg the naming of a building). They all require the recipient to acknowledge receipt of the grant, to say thank you and possibly to keep in touch on progress and to submit audited accounts once the grant has been spent. It is a constant gripe that many charities fail in these basic courtesies. A few trusts crave anonymity, and make it a condition of grant that the source is not revealed publicly.

Administration costs
Most trusts spend something on administration, to cover the cost of the administrator who is dealing with and replying to appeals, of obtaining investment advice, accountancy and audit, of producing reports and guidelines, and the cost of trustee meetings. A typical ratio of administration costs to grant income is 10-15%. This reflects the fact that it is actually quite hard to give money away!

Annual accounts
A charity is obliged to produce an annual set of accounts, which is usually audited. It may also contain a list of grants made, although the present regulations on this are not specific. Charities have to lodge their accounts at the Charity Commission regularly or when requested to do so. These are then available for public inspection. This forms the primary information source on trusts. Local trusts for the relief of poverty are under the 1985 Charities Act obliged to lodge their accounts with their local authority, where they should be available for public inspection. If the trust has not fulfilled this obligation, it must make the accounts available to the public on request, for a reasonable photocopying charge.

Appeals
A major fund-raising initiative from a charity, where the trust or donor is only asked to contribute a small part of the total. Many appeals are 'circulars', which usually end up in the bin.

Applications
A written proposal for funding. A few trusts require special application forms to be filled in.

GLOSSARY OF TRUST TERMS

Beneficial area
The geographical area within which the trustees are permitted to apply their funds. For some trusts this could be as small as a parish, a village or a town. For others it could be national or even international. There is no trust yet which has an extra-terrestrial beneficial area. Some beneficial areas are defined by ancient boundaries which may no longer exist.

Beneficiary
The persons or class of persons who can benefit from the trust. Some trusts are established to benefit *individuals* in need. Some for specific charitable purposes where grants are normally made to charitable *organisations*.

Breach of trust
Where the trustees have been negligent or have acted against the interest of the beneficiaries or operated outside the purposes and powers conferred on them in the trust deed, they are said to be in 'breach of trust'. As such they can be held liable personally to repay to the trust any money misapplied. If they have acted 'in good faith', then repayment of funds will not normally be required. This is different from trustees acting ineffectually or inefficiently. Trustees are not required to reply to outside complaints. If you have a concern about the way a trust is operating you can: (i) check the facts in the trust's file at the Charity Commission; (ii) raise the matter with the Charity Commission; (iii) seek to enter into a dialogue with the trust or raise the matter with one of the trustees; and (iv) obtain publicity for the facts (which you need to be sure of).

Charitable status
Originally defined in a preamble to an Act of Parliament in 1601, and redefined in the 1891 McNaghten classification of the four heads of charity (relief of poverty, advancement of education, advancement of religion, other purposes beneficial to the community). These purposes are continually being redefined in the light of current circumstances either through decided Court cases on charity status (the Courts are ultimately responsible for this), or through the process of registering new charities which is undertaken by the Charity Commission (in England and Wales) in consultation with the Inland Revenue.

Charitable Trusts Administrators Group
A network of trust administrators who meet to discuss matters of mutual interest. There are sub-groups on specific topics, a two-day annual seminar, and a magazine *'Trust News'*. It is proposed to merge this with the Foundations Forum (*see below*).

28

GLOSSARY OF TRUST TERMS

Charities Act
The 1960 Charities Act established the Charity Commission and charity supervision in its present form. The Woodfield Report on the supervision of charities in 1987 made various recommendations for reform which will be incorporated into a new (1991?) Charities Act. The 1985 Charities Act provided new procedures for reporting by local charities for the relief of the poor and for the winding up or merging of very small charities

Charity Commission
The body responsible for the regulation of charities in England and Wales. All but the very smallest charities are obliged to register with the Commission (with certain excepted categories), to lodge copies of their founding documents, and to file copies of their accounts regularly or when requested. This public register is used as the basis for providing information on trust activity and can be consulted by the public in London and Liverpool. There is not yet any regulation system for charities based in Scotland and Northern Ireland.

Correspondent
The person to whom applications or other correspondence should be addressed. For larger trusts this will be the trust administrator (Secretary, Clerk or Director). For smaller trusts, it might be a trustee or a firm of accountants or solicitors.

Cy pres
Certain trusts have the power to alter their objects so long as they remain charitable. But for most trusts, when the trust's objects are no longer capable of being fulfilled (when the problem has ceased to exist, or the beneficial area no longer has a population), it is possible to have the objects varied with the permission of the Charity Commission. The procedure is known as 'Cy pres', which means that the objects can only be changed to be near to the existing objects and within the spirit of the original trust. Thus the Metropolitan Drinking Fountains and Cattle Troughs Association (which still exists, providing drinking fountains in playgrounds), if it could no longer fulfil its objects, might be allowed to extend its work to cover welfare of horses or animals.

Emergency grants
Some trusts delegate the power to the Chairman, the trust administrator or a small panel to make small grants between trust meetings, where there is an urgent or emergency need for funds. These will be for real emergencies only. Otherwise all grant decisions are normally made at trustee meetings.

GLOSSARY OF TRUST TERMS

Endowment
Most trusts have assets which are gifted to them when they are founded. This is known as their endowment. If there is a specific restriction that the capital cannot be distributed but must continue to be held in perpetuity to generate an income, this is known as 'permanent endowment'. A charity's assets are normally held either in stocks and shares or in land.

Foundation
An alternative term for a grant-making trust.

Foundations Forum
A network where the leading trusts meet occasionally to discuss matters of common interest. It is intended to merge this with the Charitable Trusts Administrators Group to form a unified representative body for the trust world – an 'Association of Charitable Foundations'.

Founder
The person setting up the trust, who may or may not be one of the original trustees. The founder's intentions as to the purposes and conduct of the trust are usually expressed in the Trust Deed, and form the basis on which the trust will be run.

Guidelines for applicants
A very few trusts publish guidelines for applicants. Where they do, it is essential to read them carefully before applying for a grant – to ensure that your project qualifies and that it falls within one or other of the priority categories.

Income
Trust income derives from investment (normally in stocks, shares or property), and it is this income after deducting the administrative expenditure of running the trust that is available for distribution as grants. In the past, there was a quite rigid division between 'capital' and 'income', although this remains for trusts with permanent endowment (which are unable to distribute capital); but this division has otherwise now largely broken down.

Inland Revenue
The Inland Revenue is responsible for granting tax reliefs to charities, and grant-making trusts have to justify the grants they make as being for charitable purposes in order to obtain such relief. Where the grant is not made to another recognised charity, the purpose of the grant will have to be explained when tax relief is being sought.

GLOSSARY OF TRUST TERMS

Investment
The proper investment of trust funds is an important function of the trustees. For if the assets diminish (in real value) over a period of time, the trust will have less future income to distribute. Or if the assets do not yield a satisfactory current income, its present grant-making will be curtailed. Many trusts hold specific shares or property as a long-term investment, but others have a general portfolio. Trustees have a duty to review their investments from time to time, to take qualified advice on investment decisions, and to operate within the investment powers conferred on them in the trust deed (or failing that, via the 1961 Trustee Investments Act). Many trustees hand over the day-to-day investment management functions to advisers such as stockbrokers or merchant banks.

Non-charitable trusts
Two well-known trusts have been established for non-charitable purposes – they pay tax on their income and gains and are then able to support any project they wish, within what is permitted in their Trust Deed. The Barrow Cadbury Fund tends to support new or self-help organisations that have not or not yet got round to acquiring charitable status. The Joseph Rowntree Social Service Trust tends to support campaigning activities and has historic connections with the Liberal (SLD) Party.

Objects
The objects of the trust state the purposes for which grants can be made. For a charitable trust, these must be exclusively for charitable purposes. Some trusts have very wide objects (for example, general charitable purposes) and some have very narrow objects (for example, providing an annuity to spinsters over the age of 85 living in Sutton in financial hardship). The trust funds must be applied within the permitted objects or purposes of the trust. Trust objects can only be altered in specific circumstances (*see Cy pres*). For example if the objects are the support of widows over 75 in necessitous circumstances, grants cannot be made to widowers over 75 or to widows under 75, however necessitous their circumstances, or indeed for any other charitable purpose. If a grant is made outside the stated objects of the trust, the trustees will be 'in breach of trust'.

Policies
So long as it is within the trust's permitted purposes (*see Objects*), the trustees can at any time decide to limit the range of grants they will make. This might be a geographical limitation (only in the West Midlands, where the trust has a national beneficial area) or an activity limitation (only for bursaries for people to study their trade, profession or hobby overseas, rather than for the advancement of non-academic education). The trustees may alter the trust's policies and priorities at any time, so long as these continue to fall within what is permitted by the trust's objects.

GLOSSARY OF TRUST TERMS

Pro-active grant-making
Seeking out projects or activities for the trust to support, or supporting activities promoted directly by the trust. The opposite of 'reactive'.

Re-active grant-making
Deciding grants only on the basis of applications received by the trust. Most trusts operate in this way.

Trust
A body which holds assets for the benefit of a defined group of people. A charitable trust is a body which holds assets for charitable purposes (for the benefit of the beneficiaries as defined in the founding document). For the purposes of this book, a trust is a grant-making charity making grants to charities or for charitable purposes. Such bodies may in fact be constituted as a company limited by guarantee, a corporation or under some other legal format.

Trusts
Conditions attached to a grant of money will be binding on the recipient of the grant. These are known as 'trusts'. If the recipient is unable to spend the money for the purposes given, the grant has to be returned or revised conditions negotiated. Failure to do this is a 'breach of trust'.

Trust administrator
The person who administers the trust: who deals with applicants, prepares trustee meeting papers, supervises the investment of the trust funds and production of accounts, etc. These functions are normally delegated by the trustees who retain the ultimate responsibility for the conduct of the trust. For some trusts the administrator is a clerical assistant, for others the administrator has real power for grant decisions where his or her recommendations are normally accepted by the trustees. The trust administrator may be known as Clerk, or Secretary, or Director.

Trust Deed
The founding document for the trust which states the objects or purposes of the trust, the powers of the trustees, and the way in which the trust is to be run. For a body established as a company limited by guarantee, the founding documents will be known as the Company Memorandum and Articles of Association, which fulfil exactly the same function as the Trust Deed.

Trustee
The trustees are a group of people responsible for the running of the trust. They have two main responsibilities:
(a)The investment of the trust funds to produce an income and preserve the

capital value of the investment; and

(b)The making of payments or incurring of expenditure for charitable purposes, including making grants out of income or out of capital, or making loans. The trustees are personally responsible – individually and together – to see that the trust is operated within the terms of the Trust Deed. If is is not, the trustees would be in 'breach of trust' and be personally liable for any funds misapplied. The Trust Deed will state the maximum and minimum number of trustees that the trust should have and how new trustees are to be appointed. Where the body is constituted as a company limited by guarantee (or some other legal format), the directors of the company assume the role of charity trustees.

Trustee meetings

The trustees of a trust meet regularly to conduct the affairs of the trust. Meetings will discuss investment policy and performance, grants policy and decisions on grants. The trust administrator will usually prepare a list of recommendations from amongst the applications which have come in for decision by the trustees.

WHERE TO FIND OUT ABOUT TRUSTS

How do you set about finding which trusts are likely to be interested in your work and which trusts are never going to support you?

(a) The Charity Commission

The prime reference source on charities is the **Charity Register** kept by the Charity Commission. Although the published directories of local and national trusts will cover most requirements, the Charity Register will be of particular use in certain circumstances. The Register is comprehensive; it includes details of all trusts that are obliged to register with the Charity Commission. It comprises two parts: an index of charities, and files for each charity. This only covers charities based in England and Wales, and there are certain exceptions and exemptions from registration, particularly for very small charities. *Note:* Under the 1960 Charities Act any charity not in occupation of premises and having an investment income of £15 per annum or less was excused from registration. Under the proposals for a new Charities Act (likely to become law in 1991), any charity with a total income of £1,000 or less would be excused registration. This would mean that certain half-way house charities receiving covenant income and distributing it on behalf of the donor would then have to register. At the time of writing (1989), there was no official register of charities in Scotland and Northern Ireland, and discussions were taking place on how best to maintain public information on charities in Scotland and Northern Ireland.

The **Charity Index** is arranged in alphabetical order giving the basic details of the trust, its governing instrument, objects and beneficial area, its registration number and Inland Revenue reference, and the name and address of its correspondent. It should be noted that the Index includes all registered charities, the spending charities as well as the grant-making trusts. The Charity Register also files the information geographically by area of benefit and by subject (charities established for particular purposes). It is proposed to computerise the index during the 1990s. Although precise details of how this will be done were not available when this book was written, it is likely that the new computer-based index will contain the latest financial details and the names of the trustees.

In addition to the Index, the Charity Commission also maintains files for each charity. The file will contain the founding documents, the annual accounts (where required) and any other information that the charity has sent in. Although it is a requirement that all charities with a permanent endowment file their annual accounts with the Charity Commission and that others do so when requested, not all remember to do so. In a good many cases there is a delay in sending in the information, and the latest information available can relate to a few years ago, and may even be completely out of date.

However, where there is reasonably up-to-date information, this can give a flavour of the trust's giving over the period and a feeling of their likes and dislikes. The annual accounts for trusts making grants for charitable purposes should contain a list of the beneficiaries (except where these are individuals in need), although not all do this. There may be an annual report in addition to the accounts. Where there is a list of projects supported and grants made during the year, this gives a good indication of the scale of donation that the trust is making and which it is appropriate to apply for.

Although research at the Charity Commission can be quite time-consuming, it can be worthwhile taking time off to search through the files for a few selected grant-making trusts, where there is no other publicly available information and you believe you stand a good chance of getting a grant.

The Charity Register for England and Wales is kept in London and in Liverpool. The files are divided between the two locations, with the files for charities in the North of England (north of a line between approximately the Bristol Channel and the Wash) available in Liverpool, and for charities in the South available in London. Files can be sent down from Liverpool to London and vice versa. This requires at least one week's notice and preferably longer.

In 1989, it was decided to transfer certain functions of the Charity

Commission from London to Taunton. This will mean that files and the index can be consulted in London, Liverpool and Taunton given sufficient notice. Local charities for the relief of poverty are now required (under the 1985 Charities Act) to lodge their accounts with their local authority for public access, and have a duty to provide accounts to members of the public (for a reasonable photocopying charge) where they have failed to comply with this requirement. There is no evidence yet that this procedure is working well. For further information on how to set about researching charities, see *Researching Local Charities* (available from the Directory of Social Change).

If a charity is registered as a company it will have to file information at Companies House in accordance with the Companies Acts in addition to filing information at the Charity Commission. However, the company files are unlikely to obtain lists of grants, but they will provide an up-to-date list of directors (trustees) which are not usually available on the Charity Commission files.

(b) The Directory of Grant-Making Trusts

The **Directory of Grant-Making Trusts** is a basic reference work on grant-making trusts, which brings together information on some 2,500 trusts. It was first published in 1968 and has established itself as a major reference work for grant-makers. However, it is expensive – the 1989 edition costs £47 – but is available in most reference libraries. If your organisation employs staff and staff are being paid to consult it, it is far more expensive to spend time going to and from the reference library than it is to buy a copy. Perhaps the answer is that smaller organisations should put pressure on the publishers, the Charities Aid Foundation, to have a concessionary price available for smaller organisations.

Part I of the Directory contains a classification of charitable purposes, which includes all the principal fields of interest for the allocation of donations made by grant-making trusts. These are also listed in alphabetical order in an index. There are nine main categories: medicine and health; welfare; education; sciences; humanities; religion; environmental resources; international; and general charitable purposes. Each category is divided into many sub-categories.

Part II of the Directory lists trusts which are known to have made a donation for the specified purpose. Also indicated is whether the trust typically makes a three-figure, four-figure, five-figure (etc.) grant. If a charity is working in a particular area of work, say the preservation of historic buildings, using this section you can quickly look up the 150 or so trusts that state that they have given for this purpose.

Part III of the Directory is an alphabetical register of grant-making organisations. This gives basic information about each trust. The information is as supplied by the trusts themselves in response to a questionnaire, or where no reponse is received, from research at the Charity Commission. It is limited to trusts which have an income in excess of £1,500 per annum.

It attempts to be comprehensive, but inevitably a few important trusts and many small local trusts are missed out.

Each trust listed is asked to supply the following information:

1. Title of trust, year established and charity registration number;
2. Name and address of correspondent;
3. Names of all trustees of the trust;
4. Objects of the trust;
5. Policy of the trust;
6. Any restrictions on donations *(e.g. only to registered charities)*;
7. Beneficial area in which donations can be made;
8. Finance: income, grants made and value of assets of the trust as per the latest available annual accounts;
9. Type of grant made *(single grant, starter finance, bursaries, for specific projects, etc.)*;
10. Type of beneficiary;
11. Submission of applications *(when and how)*;
12. Publications *(stating if an annual report or other information is available)*;
13. Classification of grants *(as per categories in Part I)*;
14. Notes *(other information the trust wishes to provide)*.

Not all trusts provide the information needed to complete each section, and the information they provide may often be out-of-date, or it can on occasions be misleading. After all, no one is going to state the fact that their trust policy is to give to whichever charities take the founder's fancy; they are much more likely to tick all the categories on the questionnaire which sound socially desirable (such as medical research or environmental causes). Often the statement 'grants are made in adherence with the settlor's wishes' or 'preference is given to charities of which the trustees have some specical interest, knowledge or association' is a way of saying that the trust is one set up by an individual who still controls it, and has organised his or her charitable giving in this way as a means of obtaining the full tax advantages that are available. There is nothing wrong with this, and it at least saves charities the bother of fruitlessly having to apply.

Part IV of the Directory contains a Geographical Index of Trusts in which trusts established in each area are recorded by county and by town within each area, but note that this is by area from which the trust is run and not by area of benefit; although these may often be the same. A glaring example of how trusts can be missed using this index is the little known but extremely large 29th May 1961 Charity which is based in London, but has strong grant-making presence in Coventry and the West Midlands.

The aim of the Directory of Grant-Making Trusts is not to be an address book of trusts, but to enable applicants to make selective applications. The problem is that the accuracy of the information it contains depends on the accuracy of the information supplied by those who run the trusts. In some cases the information is no longer relevant because the trust has changed its policies; for example the trust may have been supporting environmental issues at the time it sent the information to the compilers, but two or three years later when an applicant is consulting the Directory, the trust may have switched its resources into supporting youth clubs or psychotherapy. In addition, the level of income shown for the trust may be out-of-date; trust income may rise or fall, and the figure for several years ago may not reflect the current situation accurately.

Information on size of grant is given as being 3 or 4 or 5 figure amounts. In relation to the typical size of grant there is a world of difference between £1,000 and £9,500 (both four-figure grants) and £100 and £975 (both three-figure grants). Although an order of magnitude can be inferred, the breakdown here is too crude to be of real use.

More of a problem to an applicant than the out-of-date nature of much of the information (which is largely inevitable when publishing a directory of this sort) is the misleading information put out by some of the trusts about themselves in an attempt to discourage applications. For example the statement 'trust funds are fully allocated' has become debased by misuse, and a great deal of reading between the lines is needed.

Despite these criticisms, the Directory of Grant-Making Trusts is a most useful aid when raising money from trusts. An appreciation of the limitations of the information it contains can only be helpful to applicants using it.

(c) Guide to the Major Trusts

This book was first published in 1986. The 1989 edition provides detailed information on over 420 large trusts which give £60,000 or more annually. Information is obtained from two main sources:

From the Charity Commission files, where the information is subsequently checked with the trust;

From reports, guidelines and other documentation issued by the trust (where this is available).

The Guide concentrates on grant-making practice as well as policy or intentions, illustrated with examples of grants actually made. Often these are at variance with the stated policies of the trust, and it is also possible to draw certain inferences from this information – for example, the style or approach of the type of organisation that appeals to trustees, or the fact that small local organisations are likely to receive donations of a certain size, whilst selected larger national organisations or certain activities strongly supported by the trustees might be receiving major grants.

Similar comments on the up-to-dateness of the information as for the Directory of Grant-Making Trusts apply. You should note too that grant-making practice is a reflection of past rather than present or future intentions of the trust. Although certain trusts tend to continue their policies over a period of many years, others are creatures of fashion. Seeing what they have done in the past is not necessarily a good indication of what they might ever be prepared to do.

The aim of the Guide is to provide as much information as will be useful to applicants to help them decide whether or not to approach a particular trust, and on the sorts of application that the trust might be happy to consider.

The following information is given:

1. Title of trust
2. Annual grant total and the latest year for which figures are available
3. Brief description of the trust's interests

4. Address, telephone number and contact for applications
5. Names of all the trustees of the trust
6. Beneficial area
7. Information available
8. Background and history of the trust
9. Policy and grant-making practice in detail
10. Exclusions
11. Application procedure
12. Space for the reader to insert details of previous approaches and any notes.

The annual grants total for all trusts listed in the 1989 edition was £286 million. The 1989 edition costs £12.50 and is published by the Directory of Social Change, the publishers of this book.

(d) Information on local trusts

The two directories described above concentrate in the main on national trusts, although several large local or regional trusts appear in the *Guide to the Major Trusts,* and the *Directory of Grant-Making Trusts* has details of many trusts making grants within a limited geographical area. However, for the local grant-seeker, many more trusts are in existence which are not covered in either of these books. Getting information on these local trusts can be either extremely easy or quite hard depending on the particular area you are interested in. This is because in some areas, the work of compiling a list of local trusts has already been done, whereas in others the work has yet to be done. Information on local trusts might be available from the following sources:

The local authority
Some local authorities have compiled lists of local trusts in order to encourage local grant-aided groups and projects seeking funds to look beyond getting support from their local authority. The council department which has compiled the information could be: The Central Grants Unit, Social Services, Recreation/Leisure, or Economic Development. For example in Middlesbrough, the Economic Development and Planning Department of the Borough Council has compiled a list of potential sources of funding for community economic initiatives and community business.

WHERE TO FIND OUT ABOUT TRUSTS

Charity Information Bureaux

Charity Information Bureaux are specialist organisations or units which provide information on charitable sources of funding in a region, county or city. The best established are in Birmingham, Humberside, Tyne and Wear, West Yorkshire, Wiltshire and Sussex. They research and maintain information on local trusts and maintain information on national trusts. They also advise applicants on suitable trusts to approach, trying to match projects with a trust's interest and area of benefit. A list of the main Bureaux is given below:

Birmingham Charities Information Bureau, 138 Digbeth, Birmingham BS 6DR (021-643 8477).

Humberside Community Council Resources Centre, 14 Market Place, Howden, Goole, North Humberside DN14 7JB (0430-430404).

Sussex Charities Information Service, The Chapel Royal, North Street, Brighton BN1 1EA (0273-21398).

Tyne and Wear and Northumberland Charities Information Service, 197 High Street, Gateshead NE8 1AS (091-478 4103).

West Yorkshire Charities Information Bureau, 11 Upper York Street, Wakefield WF1 3LQ (0924-382120).

Wiltshire Charities Information Bureau, Wyndhams, St Joseph's Place, Devizes SN10 1DD (0380-729279).

Many Councils of Voluntary Service *(see below)* also offer advice and help on fund-raising and keep information on grant sources, and some of these have joined the Federation of Charity Advice Services *(c/o the Wiltshire Charities Information Bureau).*

Councils of Voluntary Service

A Council of Voluntary Service or (Voluntary Action) or, in rural areas, a Rural Community Council acts as a focus for the local voluntary sector, providing co-ordination, advice and help, and a voice for local organisations. Some also organise direct services and projects. Many have a Volunteer Bureau attached to them. Inevitably these bodies are approached for help on grants and advice on fund-raising. What information they have available will vary considerably from area to area, but those which are professionally staffed should have some information on local grant sources.

Local grant guides

There are now several local grant guides available, which have collected between two covers information on local trusts. These include:

The London Grants Guide, published by the Directory of Social Change, covers all statutory and non-statutory sources for Greater London. It does not include details of London-based trusts giving money over a wider area. For information on these trusts, consult either of the national grant guides.

Merseyside Directory of Grant-Making Trusts, published by the Liverpool Council for Voluntary Service, 14 Castle Street, Liverpool L2 ONJ is a comprehensive guide to trusts in the Merseyside area.

The Wales Funding Handbook, published by the Wales Council for Voluntary Action, Llys Ifor, Crescent Road, Cardiff CF8 1XL, covers the Wales area.

Directory of Grant-Making Trusts and Organisations for Scotland, published by the Scottish Council for Voluntary Organisations, 18-19 Claremont Crescent, Edinburgh EH7 4QD. This is not comprehensive, largely because of the absence of publicly available information on charities in Scotland. However, it is the best there is for the time being, whilst future policy on charity supervision in Scotland is under review.

The Funding Handbook, published by CAFE (*Creative Activity For Everyone*), 23-25 Moss Street, Dublin 2, is a guide to money for community and voluntary initiatives in Ireland, including Northern Ireland, and has some information on trusts.

In addition, the Charities Information Bureaux in Tyne and Wear, Humberside, West Yorkshire (for grants to individuals) and Wiltshire have produced and published grant guides.

(e) Information on trusts making grants for individuals

The bulk of the information provided in the grant guides and by the charity information services listed above is for grants made to charitable organisations and for charitable projects. Many trusts exist to make grants for individuals in need or in particular circumstances. Many of these are long established (since the advent of the welfare state there has been little enthusiasm for establishing new trusts to benefit individuals) and often they are little known.

WHERE TO FIND OUT ABOUT TRUSTS

Two grant guides cover these trusts (both are published by the Directory of Social Change):

Grants for Individuals in Need covers national, local, occupational and specialist trusts making grants to individuals in need or in distress.

The Educational Grants Directory covers charitable sources of funds available to individuals for educational purposes, but does not include scholarships or other awards made for academic excellence or where the funds are tied to a particular educational institution, nor does it include details of research awards at postgraduate level.

Part 2

APPROACHING TRUSTS

APPROACHING TRUSTS

by Timothy Cook

When you are applying to trusts, there are a number of factors to be aware of which will influence your approach:

1. The size and type of trust you are applying to

The larger trusts mostly have full time secretaries/directors/clerks who are in touch with current thinking, with the social trends and social policies of the day. They meet other trust secretaries informally, and formally through the Foundations Forum, the Charitable Trusts Administrators Group and the Association of Charitable Foundations (which was founded in 1989). They know the issues of the moment that concern voluntary organisations; and they know a good deal about what is happening in the field.

Smaller trusts may have a part-time secretary or administrator. The trust may be very interested in the issues of the moment, but by the very nature of things, it is less able to keep in touch with them and to spend time in developing its policies.

Then there are the 'private' trusts; some of these are very small and some are fairly large. They tend to keep a very low profile; a solicitor or accountant may act as correspondent, and it is usually difficult to find out anything about who they give to and what they are interested in. Most usually support the charitable interests of the trustees or of the founder, rather than formulating any publicly stated policy of their own that reflects changing social needs.

Which category of trust you are applying to really determines what you say in your application. The size and type of trust you are applying to will influence not only how much you should be applying for, but also what aspect of your work or expenditure you want the trust to support, and the way in which you frame your application. So you do need to find out as much as possible about the trusts you are intending to apply to before you make your application.

Define your needs and establish your priorities

- Organisations always have more needs than can be met immediately. Decisions on priorities must be made by the whole organisation, and not by a single individual rushing into an application.

- Are trusts the most appropriate bodies to approach? There are other sources of funding available which may be more appropriate or easier to obtain: local authorities; companies; individual donations; radio and television appeals; legacies; and give as you earn schemes.

- If necessary obtain advice on which source is most relevant.

---

2. The type of application you are making

Are you making an application just to keep you going for another six or twelve months while some central government department or your local authority are making a decision as to whether they will give you a grant or not? Or are you having to raise money in a hurry because your grant has just been cut? Are you having to adjust to changing patterns in the provision of services and needing to invest in your own organisation's future to take advantage of these? Are you seeking a contribution towards your general administrative overheads? Is it a new project to add on to what you are already doing? Are you seeking the whole of the money from the trust, or just a part of it? And if the latter, where are you planning to obtain the balance? How does the proposed new funding fit in with the overall funding of your organisation? If it is a new venture, has it been well thought out, well researched and well planned? Or is it just a wild idea, something so crazy that a trust might just be prepared to support it, although you have not yet thought the idea through as thoroughly as you might? Are you an organisation that has just come into being? Or are you a well-established organisation whose work is likely to be well known?

Often the application does not distinguish between these different situations, nor does it clearly state how the project relates to what you are already doing. This is important because some trusts like to support new ideas, whilst others prefer to take fewer risks; and if your idea just catches their fancy, by showing them the wider context of your work, you might persuade them to give you a more substantial grant.

APPROACHING TRUSTS

During the 1970s and through most of the 1980s, many trusts saw their role as supporting social innovation, providing new solutions to old problems or addressing some of the newer problems facing society. In doing this, they were investing in an organisation's work in the hope that (if it was successful) the project would then be supported by some statutory source of funding and the idea would diffuse into a wider social provision. However, the financial pressures on local authorities have made it far more difficult for these innovatory projects to secure long-term funding after their initial phase. This can cause a problem for trusts, who are faced with the decision between giving continuing support to the project or being party to closing it down through lack of funds. There is no immediate or obvious answer to this. Some trusts are now prepared to give continuation funding over a longer period, some are happy to work with the organisation to develop alternative and secure sources of long-term support. If you are proposing an innovatory project, then you should at least be *considering* the longer-term funding implications and some of the avenues that could be explored when you are making your initial application.

Do your background research

- Do not guess! Try to find out the best way to approach each individual trust. Most prefer a written application. Some have application forms. Some may even prefer an initial phone call. Some may have various restrictions which must be accepted, and time and effort will be wasted if they are not.

- Research their policies and priorities: the size of their grants; who they have supported in your local area and what type of work; who to contact; and when they make decisions.

- Some trusts produce guidelines for applications - obtain these wherever possible, read them carefully and use them.

---

3. Your time scale

Some trusts consider applications annually, some quarterly, and some monthly. It is often difficult to find out when the trustees will next meet. Even where there is someone to ask, you may find that the time scale of your financial needs and the time scale that they are operating under are quite different. Some trusts have the power to give away small amounts of money virtually on request for emergencies at the discretion of the secretary or a trustee, but these are small grants for emergency purposes.

You need to be quite clear as to what your own time scale is. Did you need the money yesterday - which unfortunately is all too often the situation? Do you need it tomorrow? Or next month? Or can you state some time during the next twelve months when you will need it? Is the money you are seeking part of a general appeal (in which case the time scale will be less important)? Or will the activity not take place at all if the money is not raised (in which case the time scale is crucial)? Make your requirements absolutely clear. The trust will not normally change its way of working to deal with you, but it does establish some sort of base line around which it is possible to communicate the urgency or otherwise of the application.

Failure to do the background research

- Many trusts can produce examples from their files of organisations who have failed to do their background research. Here are some examples:

  An organisation based in London applied to the Cadbury Trusts without bothering to discover that Cadbury's only give grants to small organisations in the West Midlands.

  An organisation which worked with the elderly applied to The Prince's Trust which is restricted to supporting youth, and clearly states this.

  A church-based project applied to trusts which were not able to make grants for religious purposes. Such applications can only be supported where the project is for wider benefit.

- Often voluntary bodies apply to trusts which have an income of £10 million and ask for £100. Trusts with total incomes of £1,000 receive applications for £15,000.

Plan well ahead. Fund-raising takes longer than you think, and you will not always get the money from your first approaches. One example from my own experience is where I had applied to a trust in March; the trustees met every three months and I thought that we would receive an answer by June. In the absence of a reply, I assumed that the application had been rejected - it was one of those trusts where it was almost impossible to find out what was happening. Imagine my surprise when the following January I received a large and very welcome cheque seemingly out of the blue! In this particular case I had not mentioned when we needed the money, and perhaps they had postponed considering the application until they had the money available, or had dealt with more immediate needs first.

Raising money from trusts has now become an intensely competitive situation. Demands on trust funds far exceed the supply, and many trusts will have commitments even before they consider any new applications. You may actually be at an advantage if you do not need the money immediately. Not only will you have demonstrated foresight and good management in planning ahead, but if the trust has fully committed its present income, it may still be able to support you within your time-scale. Stating your needs helps them decide whether they can help you when you need help.

Essentials of a good application

Use the following advice to improve your application and get past the waste paper bin.

- Think carefully about your application – do not rush it.

- Be organised and concise, two sides of A4 is about right.

- Personalise the application, otherwise it looks like a general appeal.

- Try to convey a sense of enthusiasm for the project along with excitement and feeling of commitment.

- Trusts may well not have heard of your work, so your application must convince them that your organisation is well equipped to carry out the proposed project.

- Be positive and confident.

- Try to illustrate an element of self-help.

- Have your application typed if you can and, if English is your second language, then it is advisable to say so or get help in writing the application.

- If trust staff have given you advice, it is extremely important that this is followed.

- Patience and perseverance are essential qualities when applying to trusts.

---

4. How much you are applying for

It is important to know the size of donation the particular trust normally makes; you can then pitch your application accordingly. It is no good applying for £10,000 to a trust which normally makes grants of £500, and even if you could persuade it to make a grant of as much as £5,000, you would still need to be aware that you could not get all the money from this one source in order to be able to plan accordingly. Equally, applying for £500 when you might have been able to get £5,000 could be a missed opportunity, if you had a larger project for which you were looking for money, which they would have supported if only you had put it to them. And a large trust might feel that is was not their business to make small grants, leaving this function to the smaller trusts with less resources at their disposal

I have been caught out on this score both for the good and for the bad, but have usually been able to rescue the situation. Once in discussion with a trust where I was seeking support to the tune of £10-£15,000, suddenly sums of £500 were being mentioned by the other side. I had misheard my information, or perhaps I had been misinformed about how much the trust gave, or it may have been that I had allowed my fantasies to take over. A conversation where each side is mentally considering such different sums has a certain bizarre quality about it. Luckily I had not committed myself in writing, and was able to do some rapid thinking whilst sitting there in order to extricate myself. Equally, when I have been thinking of £500, sums of £12,000 have crept into the conversation. Again, I have had to re-align my thinking to provide something for the trust to suport at the level it is prepared to give.

With written applications, I am quite sure that many fail because they are pitched at the wrong level. If you have written a figure down, you have already committed yourself in writing, so it is doubly important to get it right before you write your application. If you simply ask for a 'generous contribution' rather than stating a specific sum, it makes it harder for the trust to give. You will need to do as much research as is necessary, before you sit down to write your application.

Checklist of what to include in an application:

- Background information (for example, how and when organisation began).
- Aims of your organisation and achievements in the last year.
- The scale of the organisation (for example, the numbers of your paid and voluntary staff, the quantity of work undertaken).
- Who is involved in the management of the organisation and who is responsible for policy decisions.
- Present sources of income.
- Provide evidence of need for the project.
- Spell out who will benefit from the project.
- Amount of money required and for what purposes – give a detailed breakdown.
- Correspondence address/name/phone number.
- Audited accounts, annual reports, constitution, budget for the current year. If these are unavailable you will need to explain why.

If your project costs more than you are asking the trust for, and you are only asking for a contribution towards the total, you will need to indicate how you plan to go about raising the balance. You will also need to state clearly whether you are asking for a single grant or whether you require continued support over a period of several years. If you are asking for longer-term support, you will need to think about what happens when the grant runs out. Will the project come to a natural end and be terminated? Is it a pilot project to help launch a larger scheme? If so, how do you plan to disseminate the results? Are there other sources of money which you intend to tap subsequently to keep the project going? All these need to be considered before you make your approach.

5. The manner of your approach

For most applications you will be submitting a fully thought out written application. You will have already decided which trusts are most likely to be interested in your work, and you will have emphasised the application accordingly.

In many cases this written application will be the basis on which your case will be considered, and if you are successful, you will receive a cheque in due course. For most larger trusts, and for some medium-sized ones too, the trust may want to see the applicant to discuss the application. This can be a meeting at their offices, or they may wish to make a project visit to get a flavour of your organisation and how you work. Are you expecting a meeting, and are you going to follow up the written application with a request to meet? If so, your approach will be quite different from when you approach a trust where there will be no direct personal contact. Some organisations find that their project or facilities are so attractive that anyone who visits subsequently decides to give support. In such circumstances, your aim should be to persuade people to visit you.

Are you going to try to see the trust *before* sending in your application? Some trust secretaries are prepared to see potential applicants if their work sounds interesting, although most insist on having something in writing first. If you have to send something in, you can of course submit an outline of both what you are doing and your future plans without making a formal application at this stage, and ask for a meeting to discuss the project further and to explore the possibility of funding if they are interested. Some trusts will look at draft applications and like being involved in discussing the objectives and the methods of the project. Some like being consulted about the way in which you should apply, for example whether they prefer a certain style of application and what they think you should be applying for. One danger of having extended discussions with a trust is that you get over-optimistic of your chances of success; just because they have asked you to submit something, does not mean they will fund it; and even if the trust secretary likes the project, the trustees (who actually make the decision) may not.

You must determine how you intend to approach the trust before you apply. Another thing you should decide is whether you intend to approach the most likely trust first, and if that fails then approach other possible trusts; or whether you will approach several trusts simultaneously in the first instance. If you approach trusts individually, it can take a good deal of time to work your way down the list. Much will depend on your relationships (if any) with the trusts, but certainly no harm is done in approaching several trusts at once. You should not be shy of disclosing that you are approaching other trusts as well, and you can even name them. This can be helpful. But do your homework and select the trusts carefully , and write to each one *individually* rather than sending a circular.

Features of a poor application which annoy trusts:
The following points can irritate trusts and thus hamper your chances of receiving a grant:

- Undated or unsigned letters.

- Circular appeals, especially those addressed Dear Sir/Madam (this conveys the feeling that the organisation has put in no effort).

- Asking for general donations, rather than seeking support for a specific project.

- Using out of date directories - this may result in applications being sent to dead people at the wrong address!

- Use of initials and specialist jargon unfamiliar to the reader.

- Emotional appeals based on moral blackmail.

6. What your application is about

Firstly, you should be asking for money to carry out the work you want to do. It is sometimes very tempting to see what trusts like to support, and write a perfect application pandering to their particular likes. But if you apply for money just because the money is there and you want some of it, this will ultimately reflect badly both on you and on your organisation.

You should be clear about exactly what you want to do and how this fits into your overall strategy. If you succeed in getting a grant, you will have to spend the money in exactly the way you have proposed. So what you say in the application and the costs you are budgeting to incur need to be properly thought through. This is something which should not be fudged. If there are problem areas, bring them into the open and discuss them. It is all too easy for the word to get around about the doubts people have about your organisation and the honesty of your fund-raising.

Many trusts, and particularly the larger ones, like to support 'projects', specific chunks of your work that they are interested in and can identify with. Most charities have a continuing need for money to carry out their work. They need support for core costs, the money to pay for the administration and the overheads – that is the cost of running the organisation, the office expenditure, etc. These costs are never particularly attractive for a donor to support. Dividing an organisation's financial needs up into 'projects' is a fund-raising skill that is worth acquiring. You can then allocate a proportion of the total overhead to the budget of each project. This gives the trust something to latch on to, and this can be an important ingredient of your eventual success.

Give people images of what their money will do. Link activities with their level of giving. The National Trust needs and spends millions of pounds each year. But in their fund-raising, they do not just say that they need X million pounds, but that planting a tree costs £10, or a rosebed £250, or restoring a clocktower £5,000. If someone gives £10, they can plant a tree, and if £250, a rosebed. This is all work that needs to be done, and you need money to do it. If you state specifically that the money will be spent in a certain way, then you are obliged to spend it that way. Particularly for smaller donations, if you just paint a picture of the sort of thing that a donation of a certain size will achieve, rather than state specifically that the money will be spent in that way, the money you receive can then go into your general funds. Any situation can be turned into these sorts of images: the number of children helped, the number of single-parent families rehoused, the days that the building is kept open, the sponsorship of the production of an annual report, or whatever is appropriate for your organisation.

Divide up your work into 'packages', and find trusts (and other funding sources too) that are interested in these different aspects of your work. This makes you more likely to be successful. Where you have an aspect of your work which is seemingly unattractive for fund-raising, you may have to spend a good deal of time throwing around ideas until you discover an approach which will strike a chord with a particular trust. Even if something is unattractive, you still might find someone to pay for it if you can stress its importance; for example £500 to repair the heating system may be just what one donor can afford, and he or she can see that the donation will be spent on something useful.

The trick is to highlight those aspects of your work that are important and which will be attractive to particular donors. You need to be continually creative in your thinking. Next time around the world will have changed a little. New ideas and concerns and ways of doing things will have emerged (perhaps even as a result of your work), and there will be different priorities in your work, different things to highlight in your application, different images you will give donors in your fund-raising.

Charitable status

If you intend to apply to trusts, ideally your organisation should be a registered charity. If you are not yet established as a charity, advice on how to register can be obtained from:

- The Charity Commission, St Albans House, 57-60 Haymarket, London SW1, or

- National Council for Voluntary Organisations, (Legal Department) 26 Bedford Square, London WC1B 3HU, or

- The Local Council for Voluntary Services for your area. The address for this will be in your local phone book, or can be obtained from the National Council for Voluntary Organisations.

Trusts can only make grants for charitable purposes. While most trusts only consider applications from registered charities, some are more flexible.

If your organisation is not a registered charity, it is possible to apply through another relevant registered charity.

---

7. The language of your application

You have to believe in your organisation and convey that belief to those whose support you are trying to get. The urgency and sense of infectious enthusiasm which is generated by a group of people discussing a new idea is something you have to get across. But sometimes your enthusiasm can blind you from the obvious or from thinking your ideas through properly.

Problems trusts present

Once you have overcome the various problems in applying to trusts, your problems are not yet over! Trusts present their own!

Not all trusts answer queries on the phone. Many trusts do not have paid staff.

The majority of trusts never reply to your application.

Some trusts deal with your application months after it was sent.

Another danger is that of using 'jargon' language. You may be familiar with certain words and phrases, but they may mean little or nothing to outsiders. If you cannot communicate your idea clearly and comprehensively, then it is not going to get very far. If people are unable to understand what you are saying, they will not be inclined to fund it; they may feel you have wrapped up a fourth-rate idea in fancy language just to impress them, but this will then have the reverse effect. In one application I used such phrases as 'developmental work with children' and the trust secretary asked us to rewrite the application using phrases such as 'providing toys for playgroups' and other clear and simple concepts which his trustees could understand and which made sense. More and more, and particularly with large applications, I feel that one should get someone to act as Devil's Advocate, an outsider who knows little or nothing about the work you are doing (which is the position of most of the trustees who will be deciding the application), who can go through the application and say...'You shouldn't say that'... 'I can't understand what you mean here'...'Are you sure that this will be clear to them?'...

8. Know what is going on

Trust Secretaries, particularly for the large trusts, know a great deal about what is going on. It is their business to read all the applications they are sent, to visit projects and to meet the people who are making things happen. You must know what is going on in your field, and you must also assume that the trusts know what is going on too; it can be dangerous to assume otherwise.

Maintaining impetus

To maintain impetus, you might do any or all of the following:

- Deal with queries, supply any information asked for, and answer correspondence promptly.

- Keep trusts informed of the progress of your fund-raising where you are particularly hopeful that they will support you.

- Once you have been funded, keep the trust informed of the progress of the project.

- Keep trusts on your mailing list for annual reports, attendance at open days, etc.

- Try to develop a relationship and get to know the trusts.

- If the trust secretary undertakes project visits, try to make an appointment.

- If you are asked to meet them, always turn up and be on time.

- When you are discussing your project be well briefed. Know your aims, be clear, have back-up documents.

- If difficulties develop, explain the problems immediately to the trust.

- Be honest. Don't let trusts hear about the problem second hand.

- Remember to thank the trust for their support at every opportunity; and if you receive money from a trust one year, as long as they are not confined to one off grants then consider going back in future years.

There is always the danger that when you get to the 'interview', they will ask you if you are aware of what is going on in Carlisle either because one of their trustees comes from Carlisle or because they have just received an application from a project there, and have chanced on this information. You become aware that you are not as well informed as you should be, and that perhaps you are asking for funding for something which has in fact been tried and not worked, or for something which you believe is new and innovative, but which is actually old hat.

If you do include references to other people's work in your application, you should make sure that it is relevant and not just an attempt at name-dropping. Once, I had drawn substantially on some US work and cited this in my application. The hammer fell when I was asked why I felt that the US experience was relevant in

Britain. This was not something that I had properly considered. I had felt pleased that I had made reference to this other work and shown how cosmic we were in our approach. What I had felt to be the major strength in our application, turned out to be the weakest part!

9. The length of the application

In your application you should state your case concisely. Limited and condensed information rather than an over-long, verbose application is to everyone's advantage, given the amount of paper that most trusts have to deal with and the competitive nature of fund-raising. One problem is that this can mean that you have to simplify what is in fact a rather complex project. If you say that a certain project will prevent 20 children going into care, your staff will turn round to you and say it is a much more complicated process than that. Your reply has to be that you have limited space to get the essence of the work across, and in order to succeed you have to simplify.

Most trusts are not going to be interested in the *detailed* ins and outs of one particular method of tackling a problem; and even if they are interested, they will be more interested in discussing this with you rather than reading about it in an application. You need to convey the essence of what you are proposing. The purpose of the application is to 'sell' the idea of your proposal and to secure the financial support you need to go ahead. You need to interest the trust secretary in the project and provide a convincing case for support.

Keep the application as short as possible. Cover all the essential information in not more than one or two pages; you will seldom need more than that. You may need supportive material, obviously a detailed budget, and usually an annual report and accounts to give background information about the organisation. You have to remember that most trust officers will be receiving and reading at least fifty applications every week (some fifty a day!), and that when the application is put forward to a trustees' meeting for consideration, it has had to be reduced to an even shorter precis. There are so many applications, so much paper, that it is out of the question that everything you have submitted should be photocopied and circulated to the trustees; the original application with its back-up material may be left on the table for consultation where necessary, but your very concise application will have been summarised still further for the trustees. So my advice is the shorter the better.

Some key points

- Do not sit back and do nothing. There is more money around than you are aware of, and you will only get some of it if you start asking for it.

- Keep a record of everything you do. You may leave but the charity has a continuing need for money. If you leave, make sure that the person succeeding you knows what you have done and can build on your past efforts and the knowledge you have gained.

- The key to success is persistence. Go back to them if they refuse you and tell them why they should support you, or find out what they would support, unless there is a very good reason not to do so. Create a dialogue; harass them, but in the nicest possible way.

- The right trust to apply to is the one that has already supported you. They have demonstrated their interest in your work and their support for you. You should explore the potential for repeat donations.

- A letter of acceptance is the beginning, not the end. Don't let the euphoria of getting the money blind you from all the other things you should be doing – carrying out the work you have said you will undertake, saying thank you and keeping your donors informed of your progress, and finding new sources of money for when the grant runs out are all extremely important.

- If in the end you fail, don't feel let down. There are many other sources of money, and indeed there may be many other ways of achieving your objectives at lesser cost.

---

10. Some concluding remarks

You have to make clear why you think you are the best organisation to carry out the work you are proposing, and this should not just be because you thought of it first. You should state how the work fits in with your existing programme of work, what its significance is going to be to the organisation if things go as planned, what special qualities you will bring to the project (such things as the expertise or resources at your disposal, the mobilisation of volunteers, or the link-up with other agencies or other projects elsewhere). You have a dual job of persuading the trust to fund the project and persuading the trust to fund you to carry it out.

A trust is funding the person and the organisation, as much as the idea or written application. You have to convince the trust that you are the right person and the right organisation to carry out the idea, as well as that the idea itself is good; and you have to communicate all this in your application and in your subsequent dealings with the trust. There are many good ideas around, and just because you have happened on one does not mean that you will get funding for it.

Do not pretend you have all the answers. You should be honest about this. You will never be certain of the outcome of the project, or even sure that it is going to work; and this is particularly true for anything which is in any way innovatory. It may in practice turn out to be an interesting failure. I would always be suspicious of too much certainty, especially for a new idea where by definition you cannot know the outcome. Make this a virtue, and build it into your application.

Keeping records

You need to keep proper records of the trusts you are approaching, the results of the approach and any information which will assist you in getting further support in the future. How this is done doesn't really matter. You can keep the information on a computer or on a card index, you can have a filing system for reports/guidelines and copies of applications actually sent. The basic information you require is:

- Name and address of trust
- Name of correspondent
- Date approached
- Visit or meeting and date
- Amount requested
- Response, and if positive, amount and length of grant
- Date thanked
- Notes: these could cover anything from the attitude or enthusiasms of the trust secretary to any requirement that a project that has been supported cannot re-apply for a certain period
- Further contacts: for example, invitation of the trust to attend an open day, any contacts with trustees, etc.
- Other information: any information that comes your way which will be of help to you when you decide to re-apply.

My experience of committee meetings in voluntary organisations is that at some stage someone will pipe up 'I think you should apply to trusts', as if this were some hidden source of money and, if you can get hold of it, all your financial problems would be resolved. In fact, understanding the variety of trusts that exist, getting the approach right in the different appeals you make to different trusts is very hard work and very time-consuming. Too often it is left to the last task on a Friday afternoon. This is not likely to make a successful start. I think time has to be set aside, however busy you are, to do your homework, to identify those trusts that might be interested in supporting you, to get your approach right, and generally to build up your and your organisation's credibility in the trust world.

It is a chase. Raising money from trusts is a highly competitive business. We are all desperately trying to find new angles, new approaches in the attempt to get money for our work . We are all trying to ensure that our application gravitates to the top of the pile. By definition one is likely to have fewer successes than one would like, simply because there are more of us wanting the money and rather less money (in real terms) to go round. Rather like Philip Marlowe who entered a room and said that of the three people in the room only two were dead, I take the view that of the fifty applications a trust has received, only forty-nine were unsuccessful. But I hope that I have done enough work to ensure that mine was the exception!

Editor's note: This chapter first appeared in the 1981 edition of Raising Money from Trusts, when Timothy Cook was director of Family Service Units. It has been substantially revised for this edition. Timothy Cook is now a poacher turned gamekeeper; he is Clerk to the Trustees of the City Parochial Foundation and Secretary of the Trust for London, in which capacities he is responsible for the distribution of some £4 million a year for charitable purposes in the Greater London area. Much of the advice he gives is even more relevant a decade on, when fund-raising has become even more competitive. With more organisations now seeking money from trusts, a blanket approach is even less likely to be successful, and the work you do in developing the credibility of your organisation, in researching the trust market place, and in writing a really good and relevant application to those trusts you have decided to approach will be crucial. The summarised information in the tables has been written by Alastair Cook.

Postscript: This article was first written in 1981 and though now a receiver of applications I would stand by what I wrote originally. However, some additional comments are required in the light of my experience since 1981.

Do not make assumptions about what trusts will or will not fund, but check out your assumptions whenever possible. It is clear from published information that the City Parochial Foundation may fund salaries over a three year period, yet applicants still say to me 'I assume you will not consider applications for salaries'.

APPROACHING TRUSTS

As local authority cuts begin to bite, it is unrealistic to expect trusts to step in to replace the funds lost. Some 'rescue' grants might be made or 'bridging' grants to help an organisation over a very difficult period, but longer-term replacement funding is not essentially the province of trusts.

Despite all the advice from organisations such as the Directory of Social Change, many applications are still poorly thought out and often remarkably vague. Any applicant is in competition with literally hundreds of others – undated, unsigned, circular letters addressed to the previous clerk will be looked at, but start off at a serious disadvantage. The pressure that is now on many voluntary organisations is appreciated, but a basic minimum of effort and homework is required – it is you who needs the money.

Some applicants show clearly an organisation in need of basic assistance. Rather than try to put together rushed and poorly constructed applications, it may be better to seek financial help to enable you to reach a position where you can make a more substantial application. The Trust for London has done quite a lot of work in this direction to everyone's benefit.

Timothy Cook

CHARMING MONEY OUT OF TRUSTS

by Brian Jackson

I believe that I have been successful in getting money out of trusts, when I have been able to do this, for two reasons. The first is that our team spends a lot of time getting the idea right before we ever go anywhere near a trust. We might spend a year thinking about the idea and developing our proposals before we feel that we are ready to approach trusts. Secondly, it helps when you have built some kind of track record for yourself and your organisation. This means that it becomes easier for you as you go along; and it is certainly very hard the first time getting any substantial sum out of a trust.

I'd like to take as my first example our problems in starting the Open University. The Open University scheme, on which I worked with Peter Laslett, the historian at Trinity College, Cambridge, and with Michael Young, the sociologist, who was at Churchill College, Cambridge, began for me when I read a novel by Margot Heinemann, where the hero goes to Karl Marx College, Cambridge. Cambridge has got a great many colleges, but it has no Ruskin College; it has no working class college; it has no real late-entry point. I thought how marvellous it would be if we could have a Karl Marx College in our university. I talked a lot, in fact I talked endlessly and boringly and to everybody about the idea of a Karl Marx College, Cambridge. But one day, coming down the steps of the University Library, talking to Michael Young, he just asked me why we did not do it. Instead of talking about it, I now began to think how I would actually do it. The idea was transformed from that moment on.

Then we made a mistake. We thought Karl Marx College, Cambridge would be a building like any other building; trade unionists could come up, housewives could come up, people in middle age or late life could come up; there would be short courses, week courses, week-end courses, term courses, a wide programme of activities and events. We spoke to Sir Eric Ashby, as he was then, who was master of Clare College. He became very excited about the idea and said he would present the application to an American trust. Off he went to present the application.

Nothing happened for months and months, and in the end the application was turned down. Looking back now, I realise it was a perfect example of how not to set about approaching a trust. First we acted too fast. We had not really thought through the implications of the idea, a sensible strategy for putting our ideas into practice, nor the personal consequences on us. We presented an application in the wrong way to the wrong trust; an American trust colonising Cambridge did not make sense. The only realistic funding from America for a project of this sort would have been CIA money! Also, we sent the wrong delegate. We sent a man with a title who came from a big Cambridge college. American trusts are not going to give money to him, because they think he's got millions already, and that back in Cambridge he dines off gold and silver every night. Everything was wrong. It took a great deal of time and created a lot of work.

While Sir Eric was vainly trying to negotiate, the idea began to change. Peter Laslett had just come back from the United States, and he was very excited. He had come across a university which did not have enough teachers for the amount of students it handled. To overcome this, the university had hired an aeroplane, which circled around the university all day, and was used as a television transmitter and a roving television studio. In the town below you could tune to channel 26 and pick up the lessons that were coming from the lecture hall and seminar rooms of the flying university. Extraordinary, and totally American! But it brought something else into our notion of Karl Marx College: would it not be better if the college were somehow linked to the media, combining a teaching resource with the glamour and communications power of radio or television?

Once you begin thinking along these lines, the idea becomes completely different. We had not yet seen how different it could be. Then quite fortunately, Michael Young went with the Robbins Committee to the Soviet Union (at that time we were worried about the expansion of our education system!). He spotted that the majority of graduates in the Soviet Union are taught, wholly or in part, by correspondence; this applied, successfully, to engineers and physicists, as well as people taking arts or social science subjects. It was a really quite remarkable feature of the Soviet education system.

This drew a new element into our discussions, because we had not thought about correspondence colleges. Correspondence colleges had always been considered 'below the salt'. No one had ever done any research into them; no one knew how many students they had, or what their charges were; no one knew what their results were. But despite the lack of information, it was clear that this was an unknown and potentially extremely interesting sector of education.

The whole idea was boiling up something quite differently from our original proposal. No longer were we thinking of a college attached to Cambridge University. Nor were we thinking of a residential facility. We were imagining a resource centre, with teams of travelling tutors using correspondence lessons or learning packages linked to radio or television programmes. It was at this point that we began talking to the Gulbenkian Foundation. We talked to them for a year. I should perhaps add that I have never ever received a cheque through the post without having to meet and discuss the project.

In the end, our enormous grandiose idea of Karl Marx College, Cambridge, drifted down to a builder's hut. James Thornton, who was then the Director of the Gulbenkian Foundation, told us that the Foundation would not fund buildings. The best they could do would be to pay for a caravan or something similar. After thinking it over, we went to Churchill College, which was just then being built, at a cost of millions of pounds. They had a builder's hut which they were using as the college hall. It was unbelievable: a new, twentieth century college, with the works, college silver on the table, gowns being worn, high tables and low tables, all in a builder's hut. It was extraordinary! They were waiting to move into their magnificent building which was being built around them. So we went there, had dinner, and asked the Master, Sir John Cockcroft, if they would sell us the hut (or best of all, give it to us) when they had moved out in a few weeks' time. Of course, I assumed they would give it to us. They did not; they charged £500 for it. Back to Gulbenkian, and incredibly, the trustees approved a grant for us to buy £500 worth of builder's hut. The glamour of Cambridge may have helped the grant through!

Then we found a derelict correspondence college right under our noses, the University Correspondence College in Cambridge. It was almost bankrupt. We offered to take it over. They were delighted to get rid of this dwindling educational asset for nothing. That strengthened our whole position: we now had a builder's hut and a dying correspondence college. Back we went to the Gulbenkian Foundation. The project now seemed a lot more credible; we now began to visualise putting together the project as it was being discussed with the Gulbenkian trustees.

However, we felt we needed hidden resources behind us, so we contacted the BBC. At the time, the Head of Education was a man called John Scotham. We said we had been given a correspondence college, and we had a base (we didn't tell him the details of what exactly the base was) and asked if it would be possible to set up an experiment with the BBC to see if there was a real demand for education at a distance. The proposal went slowly through the BBC committees, and the BBC eventually agreed that we could set up an O-level English and an O-level Maths series to test the demand.

Having got that little bit of co-operation, we then went back again to the Gulbenkian Foundation. You need an endless amount of time and energy, and even money, chasing trusts. The idea was much stronger now since the BBC was involved; it was almost ready to be put forward as a formal fund-raising proposal. Yet we still felt the idea needed an extra something. So what the devil could we do? We retired to the Panton Arms in Cambridge; it's amazing how much of our work was done in pubs! We felt that we'd need to have another card to push at the Gulbenkian Foundation at this point. We decided to approach Independent Television. Michael Young, who was a lawyer, did the very sensible thing of actually reading the Television Act – which I don't suppose anybody had ever done since it was passed! It turned out, in one of the clauses deep inside it, that the Authority itself could broadcast. In practice, it contracts time out to Granada, Anglia and the other independent television franchise companies, but it could also act as a broadcasting authority itself, if it so chose; it had never done so. We told them that we were working on a good idea, that the BBC was involved, that the Gulbenkian Foundation was very interested in giving financial support, that the University of Cambridge was involved and we had a base there. So what about the Independent Broadcasting Authority? They could not possibly be left out of the equation. In fact they quickly agreed to set up a scheme with us which they would call 'Dawn University'. They would let us have the television time from six o'clock in the morning until half-past seven.

We put out a first-year university programme. We found half a dozen friendly lecturers from Cambridge to give a free lecture at six o'clock in the morning, and we waited to see if anyone would get up and listen. It turned out that something like a third of a million people actually got up. It was quite amazing.

Up until now, all our work had really cost very little; there had been the cost of train fares, lunches, and the immense cost of one's own time. So far, there had not been any real investment of money. But now the package was complete, and it was at this point we formally asked Gulbenkian to put up the money, which was to be for the crucial experiment. This was to be for the National Extension College in Cambridge, which would make the idea of an Open University credible.

Our project had changed a great deal. It was no longer a Cambridge project, it was now a national project. We had moved from our original idea of face-to-face teaching in a building to this unknown field of distance teaching by radio, television and correspondence. It had become a tomorrow idea, and an idea which could be replicated on a large scale.

The Gulbenkian Trustees agreed to support the project; they gave us £30,000. With that we were able to take up twenty-six experiments with the BBC and the independent broadcasting companies, which changed the whole atmosphere about the idea of a television-based university.

Then we had an incredible piece of luck. The government called a general election. Harold Wilson was a very ambitious Leader of the Opposition at that time, he was full of the white heat of technology, and the Kennedy age and the Kennedy image. Michael Young was drafted in as speech writer. In no time at all, Harold Wilson was committed in a speech to setting up a 'University of the Air'.

That is exactly what happened. It was simply done like that. But, looking back on that, how easily we could have got it all wrong! It could have come to nothing, or gone completely awry. Thinking hard about the idea, thinking around it, turning it upside down, and spending a lot of time working on it was how we got the idea right. The rest is history.

An illustration of how right the idea is, is that at the beginning we thought the established universities were the thing to be involved with. At the end of our thinking, we had changed our minds. And our decision was right. When the Open University was first started, the Vice Chancellors of the universities were meeting together

68

regularly. They are like bishops; they call each other by the name of their university. They say: 'What do you think, Canterbury?' and 'What do you think, York?' and 'What do you think, Oxford?'. Sir Walter Perry, the Vice Chancellor of the Open University, joined them. They would not recognise him. That's a perfect example of having discovered a bit of educational territory that no one else occupied: no one occupied the airwaves and the correspondence colleges which had such potential for the provision of education. This was a perfect thing for a trust to back.

Let me take another example, to illustrate how, in our experience, an application prospers. About ten years ago, we started work with back-street babyminders. We had become more and more conscious that the pre-school question was largely turning into a middle-class question, although we were ourselves setting up pre-school playgroups (an excellent movement), and we were part of campaigns for nursery schools, which are excellent schools. But playgroups and nursery schools tended to flourish in the better-off parts of our society, where people have the time and the money and the perception to support them. They are less successful in inner city or poorer areas, and they are not very relevant to the needs of a working mother, who may be away from home from half-past seven in the morning until five o'clock in the evening. A two-hour playgroup in the church hall is not very good in such circumstances. So where does she go? Well, of course she goes to a back-street babyminder.

So how do you get a trust to support work with childminders? We could not initially see how to devise a project which would interest them. What we did in fact was as follows. A week before Christmas a team of seven of us got up at dawn, at 5.15 in the morning, in seven different large cities. We watched the arrival of children and mothers on the city streets, and recorded it as it happened. We called our project 'Dawn Watch'. I think that it is important giving a project a name, a name which encapsulates the idea of the work in a few memorable words. We found it far easier to win financial support (which we got from the Wates Foundation) because we had rolled up our sleeves and actually done something. We had looked at the question, albeit in a very humble way; we had gone and knocked on doors for follow-up interviews. I think that this specificity in the application carried a great deal of weight. The other important thing about it was that it had an element of theatre. Trusts, in my experience, are creatures of fashion and novelty to a very large extent. They often understand something better if it has this element of theatre, style, drama about it, which the 'Dawn Watch' element in that application provided.

I would like to bring in the element of failure here. I think this is a very important element which can be used to your advantage. At a later stage, we obtained support from the Chase and Gulbenkian trusts for an exercise which turned out entirely negatively. After the 'Dawn Watch' research, we wanted to do some action-research with childminders; we set up a course for illegal childminders in the Brixton area. It was the first ever initiative of this sort. It involved quite a big cost for the trusts. The minders were paid to attend; the children were looked after in a creche; the minders were taken on trips to playgroups and nursery schools; experts came down and talked on subjects such as child health.

When the project had finished, everybody was sure it had been a great success. The story was in the newpapers. The tutors were really bouncing up and down with enthusiasm for what they had done. The minders themselves felt elated and that they had learned something. As a follow-up we went back six months later and saw every minder back in her own home. We had used a measurement scale before they had come on the course, and we used it again. What we found was that six months later nothing had changed whatsoever. Everything had reverted back to where it had started. They were not looking after their children in any way differently from the ways they had before this whole event had taken place. They were not because they were still living on low incomes, had difficult husbands, were in bad housing, and so on. To change this quickly would have needed a miracle. We recorded our findings and wrote them up: a complete negative result. I have found that this degree of honesty has actually strengthened our applications subsequently.

When we first started approaching trusts, we tended to avoid the question of failure. But there is going to be a large element of failure in every project. And it is worth recording that failure as thoroughly as possible for two reasons. First of all, every trust director must know that a large number of his or her schemes either go bust or very little comes of them. It is best to face this straight. Secondly, it is very important that negative results are recorded as strongly as positive results, as the lessons learned will benefit initiatives in the future.

Let me give you one last example. We set up a 'Child Care Switchboard', a hot-line based in Nottingham, where any worried parent could ring up with any question about a child. This could be anything: careers advice, welfare rights, baby bashing, tug-of-love, the child won't talk, the child doesn't read properly. The caller would get advice, reassurance, information, contact, or even an emergency visit. We linked this project with the local radio station. The project was put to Gulbenkian, who funded it.

I noticed how much faster we had got this idea right than we had done with the Open University, and how much faster we got the money. I think this was because of three aspects of the project. Firstly, one of the jobs of trusts is, perhaps, to back people who are creating small pilot schemes which increase access to existing provision, and that was exactly what we were trying to do with this project. Secondly, instead of waiting for radio and television to come along and interview us and to invite us on to quiz programmes, we planned to go out and take over a great deal of air space. We felt that we should be aggressively approaching the media all the time, and that goes for the newspapers too, rather than let the process work the other way round. Thirdly, this project was perhaps a symbolic way of saying that we needed to re-focus our services for children. In the Maria Colwell case (and many other similar cases subsequently), the child at risk was seen by the doctor, the schoolteacher, the policeman, the health visitor, the social worker. Everybody saw that child, but the child still died because there wasn't a co-ordinated, child-based service at her disposal. Perhaps a 'Child Care Switchboard', a 'Ministry for Children' or other ideas of that sort, are steps in the right direction.

Putting this to Gulbenkian was much easier than previous applications had been. We had recorded what we had done with our previous grants in reports and working papers. You must get everything down on paper, and that is one thing that action-oriented people do not always do. As a director of a team, I find it extraordinarily hard to get my colleagues to write up their own work, as there always seems to be something more pressing for them to do. However, this is extremely important.

I have just described three success stories. But it is my belief from my modest experience that most grants that trusts give do not produce very much in the way of positive or lasting results. There is a high failure rate, and I see nothing wrong with that. It is the function of a trust to gamble and to work on the frontiers of society. If a trust does not have a high failure rate, then in my view it is not doing what its central task should be. Local government cannot afford to have a high failure rate; central government cannot afford to have a high failure rate; but trusts and foundations clearly can and should. I would now be quite open about the possibility that a project might not work. I tell the trust that if it does not work, we will write up the story of how and why the project did not work, and publish it somewhere or disseminate it somehow to get it on the record.

I now include in an application some kind of evaluation. It really is extremely important to include some kind of monitoring of every project, however simple, right at the very beginning. I know it adds more money to the costs of the project, and thus to the size of the grant you need. But if the trust you are approaching cannot manage to pay this extra cost, perhaps another trust might be persuaded to pay for that part of the project.

Also, I think even longer before ever asking a trust for a penny, because I know that it is going to take up a great deal of my time. It takes ages writing a decent application, getting the facts right, negotiating, going to see all the people you need to see. We always think twice before we approach a trust. We are really very careful to get the idea right, and to approach the trust when we feel ready. It is a waste of your time and theirs to approach when the application will fail. You should do everything you can to ensure success before asking for the money.

A final piece of advice is to introduce the person who will be working on the project to the trust. This can help enormously. They are able to see who is going to do the job, to assess their skills and competence, and to feel confident that their money will be well invested. That is all I know about charming money out of trusts!

Brian Jackson was Director of the National Educational Research and Development Trust. He died during the 1980s. This article is an edited version of a talk he gave in 1977 at a seminar on 'Raising Money from Trusts'. Many of the points he made then are even more relevant today, when there is a much greater concentration of funds and more sophisticated grant-seeking. Building your credibility with donors, taking time with the idea and getting it right, approaching trusts with those aspects of your work which they feel it is their role to be supporting, and adopting a much tougher attitude to performance and evaluation (even if this means demonstrating failure rather than success) are all points to note, whether you are a seasoned fund-raiser or just starting out.

FINDING THE RIGHT TRUST

The sheer expense of applying to trusts will dictate the need for you to be selective in the applications you write. The first stage is to sort out the sheep from the goats, eliminating those trusts which are unlikely ever to want to give to you and identifying those trusts which are the more likely sources of support. This will involve you in dividing trusts into three categories: the 'impossibles', the 'probables' and the 'just possibles'.

1. Eliminating the 'impossibles'

The first step is to eliminate those trusts which cannot or which with all certainty will not want to support you. These fall into three categories:

(a) Trusts with clearly defined objects where your proposal falls ouside the categories in which they give

Trusts are limited in their trust deed as to what they can use their funds for, just as the applicant charities are limited in their own trust deed as to the work they are able to do. If your work does not fall within what the trust is permitted to do, then there is no point at all in applying. It would be impossible for the trust to make money available for your project.

The funds of the trust may have to be applied to the benefit of people living in a particular parish or district; the trust may be limited to giving to a specific type of charitable activity, for example for the benefit of a public school or for the maintenance of a cats home. There may even be limitations on how the money is made available; for example, it may only be handed out for research or given in the form of fellowship, bursaries or prizes.

(b) Trusts with clearly defined policies where your proposal falls outside their present policies and priorities

Trusts are also limited by what the trustees want to do. So even if it is possible for the trustees to give to your project under the terms of the trust deed, the trustees may not be willing to give to you because you are not the sort of activity they wish to support. Many of the larger trusts have clearly defined policies. The trustees decide the area of work they are interested in and the sorts of project they will fund. Sometimes they will make the information public in published guidelines or reports. Sometimes no information is available, and you will have to deduce their policy from the sorts of grants they have been making in the past.

Unlike the trust's objects (which cannot be changed unless they are incapable of being fulfilled), the trust can change its policy at any time. So even if it is not trust policy to support your area or work at the present time, the trust might extend its policy at some later stage. This might be particularly true where you are active in a field of emerging social concern such as AIDS or the environment. For example, the Laura Ashley Foundation in 1989 decided to change its policy from second chance education and overseas projects to giving support for the environment. It is worth keeping in touch with what trusts are up to through the various journals and trust directories, and by keeping your ear close to the ground.

(c) Trusts which give to charities known to the trustees

Many trusts have no policy at all. They have been established by an individual who has made money or wishes to indulge in 'philanthropy', and has established a charitable trust as a vehicle for his or her giving. This sort of trust will normally only give to those projects, organisations and appeals that the person setting up the trust (who may not necessarily be a trustee) wishes to support. This sort of trust does not welcome applications, and will not normally read them or respond to them. They are solely the charitable account of the individual, set up in the form of a trust in order to take advantage of the tax advantages that are available on charitable giving. They give to what they wish to support and what they have always supported (anything from a contribution to a public school appeal, to annual donations to the local boys club, scout group, church, or national animal charity). They give for a hundred and one idiosyncratic reasons, and unless you have a personal contact with them, you are unlikely to elicit their support for your project. It is often impossible to find out anything about these trusts. The correspondence address is probably only that of a solicitor or accountant.

2. Drawing up a list of the 'probables'

Having eliminated the impossibles, you are then left with a large number of trusts which are potentially able to give to you. The next stage is to identify those trusts which (you believe) are likely to be interested in what you are doing and might, therefore, be persuaded to give to you.

(a) Trusts which have supported you in the past

The most valuable asset in your possession is your existing donor list; this also includes trust donors. The trusts that have given you money in the past have demonstrated that they are sympathetic to your cause and that they are interested in your work. The potential must be there to get further money (except where they have a stated policy of not supporting organisations which they have funded in the past). You must take care not to alienate past donors – this can be anything from a failure to say thank you to mis-spending the money that they have given you. But more than this, it is important to do what you can to keep them on your side. Tell them what has happened with the money they have given you; invite them to your premises; send them reports and copies of any other information you produce. The emphasis of getting the money often blinds you from all the other things you should be doing to keep in contact and encourage further support. Your past supporters are all a potential source of future support; the first cheque you receive can be the start of a long-term relationship.

(b) Trusts with policies and priorities which match what you are proposing

Where a trust has a specific policy or focus on your area of work, then it should be put on your 'probables' list. This does not mean that they will want to support the application you are about to send out, but at least there is some common interest.

You would have to think quite carefully about whether yours is the sort of project they are likely to support. Do you fit within their current priority categories? Would they prefer to fund local or national projects? What types of grant do they make and for what purposes? Does your organisation have the credibility to be given support? And if not, would it be better to wait awhile or to seek a smaller grant now?

You should also try to draw links and build connections between what you do and those particular activities that they are interested in. If you undertake arts activity and they are interested in facilities for the disabled, for example, then there will be an overlap of interest for the installation of facilities for the disabled.

(c) Larger general purpose trusts

Some of the larger trusts have no actual policy as such, but give over a wide range of charitable activity. Your project might just catch their fancy, and if they are large, they certainly have the funds to support you. On this basis it may be worth putting them in the 'probables' list.

(d) Local trusts

Where you are a local organisation, or a national organisation seeking support for a local project, then the local connection becomes extremely important. Local trusts fall into three categories:

(i) Trusts with a specific local brief to support projects in the area. These can be large or small, long-established or just set up, trusts which fund projects or which support individual need. In every area there will be a whole range of trusts which give support locally.

(ii) Larger trusts based in your area where their presence on your doorstep makes it more likely that they will know of you, be interested in your work and be able to visit you to see what you are doing. The Wates Foundation, for example, gives some preference to projects in South London.

(iii) Smaller trusts without any specific local brief, where the local connection might be an additional factor in persuading the trust to give support.

Local trusts are extremely important. Because their geographical brief is so limited, there is really quite a good chance of getting support. It is also worth thinking about the type of support they are likely to want to give. A smaller trust will only make small grants, perhaps towards a piece of equipment or an activity that is obviously a good thing (such as an old people's outing).

(e) Trusts where you have some form of personal contact

It is always said that fund-raising is more about who you know than what you know. Many trusts give to projects or to organisations that are known to them. These are normally different from those trusts with clearly stated policies, although, even here, personal contact will be helpful. The importance of personal contact in fund-raising cannot be underestimated. You might know the founder of the trust, the Chairperson or one of the trustees, the trust administrator or the correspondent. Or one of your colleagues, trustees or patrons might have a useful contact.

You yourself do not need to be amongst the good and the great to have contacts. For example, the fund-raiser for a youth training project in the St Paul's area of Bristol had been at school with the son of the senior partner of a local firm of accountants which administered three larger Bristol trusts, and a Bristol city farm worker had shared a flat with a trainee at a firm of management accountants that administered two further local trusts. These contacts could be used to develop points of personal contact.

It is worth considering an 'audit' of the contacts you already have, and then to consider how these might be used to your advantage in your fund-raising.

Where you think that a trust will be interested in the sort of work you are doing, you can either send an application to them without further ado, and if it is not exactly what they want to fund, you can then try to enter into a dialogue with them subsequently. Or you may want to talk to them informally first, before submitting a detailed application. Many of the larger trusts have full-time secretaries, most of whom are very approachable. You could telephone (although most of them profess to hate this as it interrupts them), or you could write to them very briefly outlining your work and asking if it is the sort of thing that their trustees would be interested in supporting. Interpret their replies with care – they are all inclined to be discouraging for fear of misleading applicants or giving them a sense of over-confidence.

It is often useful, and it can be a pretext for contacting them in the first place, to ask how long an application to them should be, the sort of information they would like to see in it, and the level of funding they normally give. This last point is important, because you do not want to apply for too little or too much; you do not want to suggest something that is way beyond their means on the one hand or pitch your application far lower than they might have been prepared to support on the other, nor do you want to spend a great deal of time preparing an elaborate application to what is a potentially very small donor. When asking trusts how much they give, one feels like the man who went to the bank to ask for a loan; when the Manager asked how much he wanted, he replied 'How much have you got?'. If only you knew how much they would give and what for, you could find something from what you are doing that would meet their requirements!

If the trust does not want to give towards running costs, and many prefer to give to 'projects', you have to break what you are doing into coherent chunks of work or items of expenditure that they can support. If, for example, you know that the trust is sympathetic to children, then you could isolate those aspects of your work involving children and make a coherent case for support for this aspect of your work. Make sure that the information you have is as up-to-date as possible. It is no good making a case based on their last year's preferences, only to find that they have changed their policies. Trusts shift ground all the time. If you were a fly on the wall at one of their meetings, you would know how their thinking was changing and be able to pick up on all their prejudices and idiosyncracies. But as you are excluded, you have to find other means of discovering what is going on.

Once you have identified points of common interest with a trust, you need to work on them often over a long period of time. Often your initial application is turned down, but do go back. This is an extremely important point which cannot be stressed strongly enough. You have done all the research and know that they are one of the trusts that are most likely to support you. Ask why they have rejected you; create a dialogue; ask if there is any chance if you resubmit, or if they would be interested in any other aspect of your work. This may take nerve, but fortune favours the brave!

On a lot of occasions you might be applying to the right trust, but at the wrong time. They may be turning down your application because they have allocated all their funds for the time being, or because they just want you to keep trying – you may be a new name to them or be doing something that they have not yet considered supporting, and if you show persistence and go back next year or the year after, they may in fact support you.

The important factor from your point of view is not to spend too long preparing an application which is not likely to succeed. It may be appropriate to spend a week on an application which might yield a £20,000 grant; it is not sensible to spend a week on an application which is only likely to get you a £250 donation. This applies to trusts where you have very little information about what they do, and it also applies to trusts which you know may be interested in your work, but only give relatively small donations.

3. Dealing with the 'just possibles'

This category includes the large number of trusts which could potentially give to you, but where you have no indication that there is any particular reason why they should actually do so. You will only find out which of these are interested in supporting you if you approach them. But since your chances of getting money from any one trust are slender, and even if you do succeed you are not likely to get a very large sum of money, your approach to this category of trust will necessarily be less specific than for the larger trusts.

For these smaller trusts, a blanket mailing approach will normally be most appropriate. The funds of these smaller trusts may be very limited or they may give mostly to projects and organisations they know well, but it could be that your appeal might just take their fancy. They may have read about you and the problems you are dealng with in the Daily Telegraph that morning, or it might be (unknown to you) that they know one of your trustees.

It is possible to make your blanket mailing not appear as such, but to design it in such a way that it gives the impression of an individual approach. A nicely printed appeal letter individually topped and tailed, and perhaps with the name and address of the recipient typed in, using the same typeface, accompanied by a brochure or annual report, need not be expensive and can be very effectively done.

Much as some trusts fume against general mailings and say that they consign every circular to the wastepaper basket unanswered, there are still instances of successful circular appeals. And even if you pick up only a few thousand pounds, this can still be cost-effective if you have spent only limited time and effort on the approach. It is money you would not have otherwise raised, and you will have the names of a few more trusts to add to your donor list. In the absence of any better information from trusts, it is still worth this sort of approach if you feel your project at least stands a chance of being supported.

Every trust is a recipient of public money through its tax-exempt status. It is well within your rights to remind them of the pressing problems of the world as you see them and to tell them that you exist. Even where a trust is essentially a private fund, the money must be used for the public good: and they do not want to receive appeals from any particular type of charity, the least they can do is to make their donation policies clear to the people who are raising money for charity.

4. Approaching overseas trusts

Overseas trusts are a largely unexplored source of funding. In part this is due to lack of knowledge, but in part due to the limited circumstances in which an overseas trust would be interested in funding work in this country.

There are overseas trusts that have been established to provide funds for projects in this country: perhaps the best known is the Lisbon-based Gulbenkian Foundation which has a separate UK Branch with its office in London. Another such is the Dutch-based Bernard Van Leer Foundation, which operates in the UK through a separate UK trust. The Oak Foundation is an international foundation which happens to be based in London. These are all listed in the *Guide to the Major Trusts* and *Directory of Grant-Making Trusts*.

Most often an overseas trust will be interested in work being done in its own country, or in international issues of wider concern, or in supporting aid and development work in the poorer countries of the world. Some of the situations in which an overseas trust might be interested in the work of UK charities include:

Work of international significance;

Cross-cultural studies or trans-national projects where the trust is situated in one of the countries concerned;

The replication of a project or idea originally started in the country where the trust is based, or where the outcome of the project is likely to be of significance where the trust is based;

Overseas visits and study tours;

Where there is some historical or other link between the project and the trust or the country where the trust is situated.

It is up to the applicant to develop points of contact and elaborate on the reasons why an overseas trust should provide money for work in this country. Since it will normally be easier for a British charity to obtain money from a British trust, the scope for exploiting home sources of money will be far greater than looking overseas.

There are a number of directories which list overseas trusts. These are all expensive to purchase, and some may need translating. Some may be found in the reference libraries of the Charities Aid Foundation (London office: 18, Doughty Street, London WC1N 2PL, tel: 01–831 7798, which is also the UK reference point for the US based Foundation Center), or the National Council for Voluntary Organisations (26 Bedford Square, London WC1B 3HU).

For international relations projects, an analysis of overseas foundations is included in *Peace and Security: a guide to independent organisations and grant sources* which is published by the Directory of Social Change.

WRITING A FUND-RAISING PROPOSAL

Once you have decided which trusts are likely to be interested in your work, you will have then to approach them. Your initial approach may be via a phone call requesting a meeting, or you may send something in writing. At this stage you may only want to discuss an idea-in-progress to get the trust's reactions and comments, or you may want to make a formal application for money. Whatever your approach, at some stage the trust will want a proposal in writing. A few have application forms to be filled in, but most simply require a letter of application or a proposal with a covering letter.

It is not only your written proposal on which you will be judged. Assuming your project is a good one, there are two other ingredients which will contribute to your success:

Your reputation: trusts back people and organisations as well as ideas. If they do not know of you, they will often try to find out as much as possible on the informal grapevine and occasionally consult advisers. What you have done in the past, whether you are known as someone who has done good work and someone who is known to deliver the goods will all be important.

How you come over: particularly if you are applying for a large grant, the trust secretary will probably want to meet you to discuss

---

A logical structure for an application

• Introduction

• Problem statement/assesment of need

• Objectives for the project/what you plan to achieve

• Methods/how you propose to do it

• Budget/what you need to do it with

• The request/what you are asking for

---

the proposal in greater detail to clarify any outstanding points and to gain an overall impression of you and your organisation.

However, the written proposal is extremely important in sparking off interest and persuading the trust to back you. It can be their first point of contact, particularly if you are new to fund-raising as most trusts prefer a first approach to be in writing. A good, well-written proposal will improve your chances of success. Besides stating what you plan to do and how much you require to do it, your proposal has to communicate two further things: firstly a sense of urgency and immediacy, that your project is important and worth doing; and secondly that your proposal is realistic and that you will be able to achieve your objectives.

There is a danger that you will provide too much information. The trust secretary reading your proposal will be receiving perhaps ten or twenty applications a day (or even more). Some can be rejected immediately because they are inappropriate for the particular trust (they may be outside the trust's area of interest, or beneficial area, or they may be a circular appeal, or whatever). But the bulk of the applications will be read or at least glanced at – and that is a lot of reading. If you can put your idea and your case for support into as few words as possible, it will not only help the trust, but it will also demonstrate that you can think clearly and concisely. The length of your application will depend on who you are applying to and on how much money you require. As a general rule you should try to fit an application to a trust into no more than two pages plus any supporting material (the budget for the project, accounts, plans or photographs, endorsements, etc.). This is not to say that if you write a much longer application, it will not succeed; but there is no point writing a 12-page application where a one or two-page one will do. It may seem odd that only a few pages are required to get a large grant; but it should be remembered that the trust is not paying for your written effort, but it is paying you to carry out the work you have outlined in your proposal.

Besides the tendency to be over-verbose and go into unnecessary detail, there is also the problem that you are so close to the idea which you have been formulating and developing over many months, that you may not be able to write a balanced application – you may have left out something that is extremely important because something else is of great concern to you at the time; or you may have gone into unnecessary detail on something that is peripheral and perhaps should not even be mentioned in the application; or you have used jargon which is unintelligible to anyone not directly involved in the work. The answer is to get an outsider to read your application and comment on it, to tell you what is unclear and what is unnecessary, and thereby help you improve your proposal.

There are no golden rules for writing a proposal. It is very much a matter of personal style and temperament. What works for one person will not necessarily work for another. And what works for you is what you should pay attention to. You may very well be able to get away with a piece of rhetoric or an impassioned plea for funds in your own handwriting, or a very brief statement of your plans. The suggestions that follow are meant as guidelines only. You can reject all of the ideas or pick up on those that seem important to you. What is important is that you should write an application that you are happy with and that you feel you can persuade someone to support.

Whatever the form of the proposal you actually produce, it has to fulfil certain functions. It has to inform the reader of who you are and what you intend to do, and it also has to say how much money you need and what you intend to spend it on. And it should do this in a clear and logical way. Some of the elements you might use in constructing your proposal are detailed below:

Title
It is often a good idea to give your proposal a title, particularly if you can do this in a catchy phrase which captures the essence of what you want to do.

Summary
For a longer proposal, a summary can be very important. It presents the essence of what the proposal is about, and allows the reader to determine whether it is likely to be of interest. The summary may be presented as a covering letter, or the first paragraph of the application letter itself. It should be clear, concise and specific. It should describe who you are, the scope of your project, and the projected cost. The summary is the first part of your proposal that will be read, and it may be the last!

Introduction
This is the section of a proposal where you say who you are. Many

proposals tell little or nothing about the applicant organisation and speak only about the project or programme to be conducted. If you are a nationally known organisation, you can state who you are in a line or a sentence. Most organisations will need to provide a good deal more information than this. More often than not proposals are funded on the basis of the reputation of the applicant organisation and its key people, as well as on the basis of the proposed project. The introduction is the section in which you build your credibility as an organisation which should be supported.

What gives an organisation credibility in the eyes of a funding source? Well, first of all, it depends on the funding source. A traditional, rather conservative funding source, will be more responsive to persons of prominence on your board of trustees or directors; it will also take into account how long you have been in existence, what your public image is, what other funding sources have been supporting you, and other similar characteristics of your organisation. A more 'avant garde' funding source might be more interested in the community involvement in the project rather than any prominent people who are associated with it, or in organisations that are new rather than well-established, in how pioneering your past work has been, etc.

Remember the credibility in your introduction may be more important than the rest of your proposal. Build it. This is something that should be done continuously, and not just when you find yourself short of money. This requires a continuing development of your contacts with trusts, good public relations, and an ability to tell people that you really are doing a good job.

Potential funding sources should be selected because of their possible interest in your type of organisation or your type of project. You can use the introduction to reinforce the connection you see between your interests and those of the funding source.

Here are some of the things you can say about your organisation in your introductory section:

What previous connection with the funding source you have had in the past. Whether you have had a grant before, or applied and been turned down.

Your organisational goals or objectives and the basic thrust of your work.

How you got started.

How long you have been around.

Anything unique about the way you got started, or the fact that you pioneered a new type of activity.

Some of your most significant accomplishments as an organisation, or, if you are a new organisation, some of the significant accomplishments of your staff in their previous roles.

What support you have received from other organisations and prominent individuals (accompanied perhaps by letters of endorsement which can be put in an appendix).

Maintain a 'credibility file'. In this file you can keep copies of newspaper articles about your organisation, letters of support you receive from other agencies and from your clients. Include statements made by key figures in your field or in the political arena, that endorse your kind of programme, even if they do not mention your organisation. And use this information creatively in writing your proposal.

Problem statement or assessment of need
In the introduction you have said who you are. From the introduction the trust will know your interests and the fields in which you are working. Now you will home in on the specific problems that you want to solve through the project you are proposing.

There are some common pitfalls into which groups fall when they try to define problems. Sometimes an organisation will paint a broad picture of all the ills plaguing people, the community or the world. They do not narrow down to a specific problem or problems that are solvable, and they give the trust the feeling that it will take a hundred times the requested budget even to begin to deal with the problems that have been identified. This is overkill. It often comes from the conviction of the applicant that it must draw a picture of a needy community in all its dimensions in order to convince the trust that there really are problems there. All that this does is to leave the trust asking 'How can this organisation possibly hope to deal with all of those problems?'

Narrow down your definition of the problem you want to deal with to something you can hope to accomplish within a reasonable amount of time and with reasonable resources.

Document the problem. How do you know that a problem really exists? Don't just assume that 'everybody knows this is a problem...'

That may be true but it doesn't give a trust any assurance about your capabilities if you fail to demonstrate your knowledge of the problem. You should use some key statistics here. Do not fill your proposal with tables, charts and graphs. These will probably turn off the reader. If you must use extensive statistics, save them for an appendix, but pull out the key figures for your statement of the problem. This can be far more effective than dealing in generalities and using words such as 'desperate' or 'urgent' or 'unique', which become meaningless if read in a hundred applications.

You need to do the following:

Make a logical connection between your organisation's background and the problems and needs with which you propose to work.

Support the existence of the problem by evidence. Statistics are but one type of evidence. You may also get advice from groups in your community concerned about the problem, from prospective clients, and from other organisations working in your community and professionals in the field.

Define clearly the problems with which you intend to work.

Make sure that what you want to do is workable – that it can be done within a reasonable time, by you, and with a reasonable amount of money.

Objectives

An objective is a specific, measurable outcome of your project. Clearly, if you have defined a problem, then your proposals should offer some relief of the problem. If the problem which you identify is a high incidence of vandalism by young people in your community (substantiated, of course) then an objective of your programme should be the reduction of the incidence of vandalism among the youth in your community. If the problem is unemployment, then an objective is the reduction of unemployment.

Distinguish between methods and objectives. If you are having difficulty in defining your objectives, try projecting your organisation a year or two into the future. What differences would you hope to see between then and now? What changes would have occurred? These changed dimensions may be the objectives of your programme.

It is worth examining your objectives in a little more detail. Maybe some programmes create jobs for people that are very temporary in nature, and even if they reduce the unemployment problem in the short term, after a year or two the problem will be back, as bad or worse than ever.

You should be concerned about the quality of your work as well as the quantity. But you should still be precise in what you intend to achieve, rather than vague. In this way you can demonstrate a cost-effectiveness and that your project represents value for money. Many grant-makers are now judging applications on the 'value' for the money they are putting up. They want to see their money producing a real impact.

Methods

By now you have stated who you are, the problem you want to work with, your objectives (which promise a solution to or reduction of the problem) and now you are going to explain how you intend to bring about these results. You will describe the methods you will use – the activities you will conduct to accomplish your objectives.

The informed reader may want to know why you have selected these methods, particularly for an innovative project. This requires you to know a good deal about other projects of a similar nature. Who else is working on the problem and where? What methods have been tried in the past, and are being tried now, and with what results? In other words, can you justify or substantiate your approach?

Budget

The budget is a statement of what you intend to spend. This will include: payments made to staff, together with pensions and National Insurance contributions; an allocation for rent, rates, maintenance, insurance, heat, light and other office costs; the costs of postage, stationery, duplicating and telephone; expenses on travel, publications, training courses and so on; publicity; producing interim and final reports. The cost categories you will need to include in your budget will depend on the precise nature of your project.

An important cost that is often omitted is central overheads. If the project is just one of a number of activities being undertaken by a larger organisation, there will be a number of indirect costs which can be justifiably apportioned to the project. These include an allocation for the time spent by the director and his staff in getting the project under way and overseeing it, and other aspects of central administration such as management committee meetings, personnel and the accounts. Very often it is far easier to get money for projects than it is to cover the central administration costs, and one way round this is to allocate the central administration costs over the various projects being run by the organisation, and build them into the project budget. You also may want to include a contingency item to cover unforeseen costs.

Another problem is inflation. There are two ways of tackling this. Firstly, you can allow for inflation at a guessed rate; secondly you can compute your own budget at present costs and ask for an inflation allowance to be added for each year according to the prevailing level. If you are in doubt, consult the trust as they may have specific guidelines for applicants. No funding body wants to jeopardise a project by not raising its grant to keep pace with inflation, but inflation has put pressure on them as their disposable funds may not have been rising as fast.

Be realistic in your costings. Put in everything you think you will in fact spend. If you understate your financial needs, you will only cause trouble for yourself at a later stage. If the amount you need to raise seems too horrifyingly large, then perhaps think of other ways that you might tackle the same objectives, but with a smaller budget. If you are only applying to a particular trust for part of the money you require, you should state where you intend to obtain the balance, whose support you are seeking, and whether you have had firm indication as to whether it will be forthcoming.

Finally it is a good idea to try to get hold of budgets for similar projects to the one you are proposing. In this way you will see whether you have included everything you ought. You will also be able to compare your cost-effectiveness.

Another extremely important consideration is what you intend to do when the grant you are seeking runs out. Is your project something that has a fixed life; or, if it is a continuing project, what are your future funding plans? You need to think about this at the outset, as no trust wants to be locked into supporting a project for ever. One way used to be to get a commitment from a statutory authority to take over the project once it had proved itself; but with the cutbacks in public spending, this has become increasingly difficult, if not impossible. If you cannot get any actual commitment, then you can at least indicate how you plan to arrange your future funding; it may be with some statutory support, or you may be able to generate funds through the project itself, through such things as earnings, or general fund-raising activities, or membership subscriptions. You may not indeed be certain that you will be able to obtain funding in the way you suggest, but at least you will have thought about the problem at an early stage and provided some reassurance to those who would like to fund you.

Presentation

Mosts trusts prefer and respond better to a personal application. This can mean that the application is individually typed, or you can design it so that a photocopied proposal which is sent to several trusts is accompanied by a personal covering letter to each trust which outlines the project and why it might interest them, particularly. Applications which look like circulars tend to be discarded.

The way you present your proposal is important. It should certainly be neatly typed on writing paper of a reasonable standard. If you do not have suitable office equipment, there may be several organisations in the vicinity who are prepared to let you use theirs. The content is obviously more important than the presentation, but your application has to be readable and has to compete for attention with a large number of others. If it is neat and tidy this gives an impression of competence, but note that the converse is true also.

Your aim should be to produce something which looks personal and which relates to the interests and concerns of the funding source, but which at the same time is cost-effective for you to produce. A word processor can be extremely useful here as it allows you to standardise a good deal of the proposal, whilst including the particular information that is relevant to that trust. But if possible, make it look as if it has been typed. A typewritten proposal which looks as if it has been word-processed may fare less well than a word-processed proposal which looks as if it has been typed.

For circular appeals, it is worth going to the bother of 'topping and tailing' – typing in with the same typewriter face the name and address of the trust you are writing to and a salutation. Make sure that this is properly aligned. Letters which begin 'Dear Sir', or 'Dear Sir or Madam,' will not get very far.

For all appeals, it is sensible to avoid a too glossy apearance. If you seem to be wasting money, you are not likely to get it. An exception to this rule is the large, prestigious appeal, where glossy material is acceptable and even expected. If your brochure or report *appears* expensive, try to get it sponsored and bring this to the attention of the reader.

Key points

The main points to remember in any application are:

Build the credibility of your organisation;

Support the need for your proposed project;

Develop clear, specific, measurable and attainable objectives;

Justify your approach;

Include methods for evaluating your progress;

Show how your future funding will go;

Use simple, clear, understandable language – avoid jargon and rhetoric;

Say it concisely and briefly;

Prepare a realistic budget for all your costs;

Pay attention to presentation.

A fund-raising proposal is part of the process of selling an idea to people who will support it. It is a means of getting money, but it is a plan for what you intend to do with the money too. Just as with an architect's impression of a proposed building, you will seek to show your idea in the best light and to highlight its virtues whilst playing down its weaker points.

The proposal and project are in fact two separate things and it is as well to pause here and consider. If you write a poor application for a good project, you do nothing to improve your chances of getting the money; and you will certainly do better if you were to write a better application. If you have written a good application and what you have written is what you intend to do, then you have done well enough; the funding agency then has to select what it feels to be the most interesting or most deserving projects from the applications it has received. If you have written a brilliant application, but this does not reflect what you intend to do, then that is something of a confidence trick; you may get the money. But if anyone finds out that you are not doing what you said you would do, then the reputation of both you and your organisation would suffer.

There is a twin danger in proposal writing – for the written description to diverge from the reality of the project it is describing, and for the applicant to orient everything towards getting the money and towards the quirks of the particular funding body at the expense of doing what they want to do.

There is also the danger of indulging in easy hype. If for example you want to start a tenants' association on a housing estate and you have described the proposal as 'a breakthrough in housing management; potentially the most effective solution to vandalsim and disrepair since...', you still have to start the tenants' association and keep it running and to put enough effort into the work to get the results you have described for it. It is up to you to do the work, and that is the job of your organisation. The fund-raising application is the means of achieving that goal, a necessary pre-requisite and perhaps the easiest part of the process.

Dissemination

Different fund-raising projects have different outcomes. A building may be built or a piece of equipment purchased... in which case the funder will need to be assured that there will be sufficient funds to run the building or operate the equipment, and this needs to be shown in the proposal. If the money is to undertake research or produce a publication, the funder will need to be told how the research will be disseminated or how the publication will be distributed. If the money is for some form of innovation, a traditional role for trust funding, then the funder will want to be shown how the success of the project will be measured and what will be done subsequently to promote the lessons learned.

The application for funds is just the first part of the process. Obtaining the money and undertaking the work outlined in the proposal is the second stage. A third stage is to make use of the outcome in some way, and where this is an important ingredient of the proposal, it should be fully discussed in the application.

Evaluation

Increasingly funders are wanting the organisations they support to produce some sort of evaluation of the outcome of their work. There is a move away from the concept of 'subsidy' to the concept of 'investment', and investment implies some form of quantifiable return for the money spent.

This means setting measurable objectives for your project and then measuring the results you achieve, whether you are measuring the number of people attending your activities or changes in attitude or behaviour towards the problem.

This will not only demonstrate how effective you are – and if you can do this you will find it that much easier to obtain funding in the future – but it will also provide you with a tool to manage your project, to make the appropriate changes and adjustments as the work proceeds.

Evaluation can cost a good deal of money – for professional consultancy, for surveys and other market research, and for the work involved in the measurement of outcomes. From time to time, it may be appropriate for an organisation to undertake a serious evaluation with the aim of setting the stage for its future development. Indeed the costs of this can be packaged up into a 'project' which trusts might find attractive to support. But evaluation need not cost money, if it is thought through and built into the way the project is run. Evaluation of what you do shows a professional approach, and in a competitive world, this can only be an advantage.

During 1988, the Home Office Voluntary Services Unit and the Forbes Trust sponsored a programme of research and discussion of the importance of evaluation in the voluntary sector, the circumstances in which it might be appropriate, and some of the tools that can be used. A publication *Evaluation in the Voluntary Sector* and reports of the various seminars that were held are available from the Forbes Trust.

Charitable status

Most grant-making trusts are charities, which means that they must apply their money for charitable purposes only. What is charitable is defined in the preamble to the 1601 Statute of Elizabeth, updated in the 1841 McNaghten rules which categorised charitable activity within four 'heads of charity': the relief of poverty; the advancement of education; the advancement of religion; and other purposes beneficial to the community. What is held to be charitable is determined within the framework and by decided case law where decisions have been challenged in the courts, and by what the Charity Commission (in England and Wales) and the Inland Revenue will accept as being charitable.

A trust can make a grant to a charity, but it can also make a grant to an organisation which is not a charity *provided that the money is spent for charitable purposes.* Some trusts are restricted to making grants only to organisations that are charities by their trust deed. Others do so as a matter of policy because it is simpler administratively (they do not have to explain the purpose of each grant when making their returns to the Inland Revenue).

If your organisation is not a charity, then it may be possible to make an arrangement with another organisation (which is a charity) to receive the grant on your behalf and pay it over to you. The receiving organisation should have compatible aims and objects with your own organisation and also have the power in its own trust deed to make grants. Typically you might contact a local Council for Voluntary Service or a Regional Arts Association to act in this capacity.

If your organisation is not a charity, you should make these arrangements *before* you start to apply to trusts, and you may wish to indicate the mechanism for paying over the grant in your application.

Sending off your application

One common difficulty people have is planning how, when and to whom to send off their applications. They may have targeted a number of potentially interested trusts and need several grants to make up the total cost of the project. Which trust should they approach first? And for how much? How can they maximise their chances of meeting their fund-raising target? And how can they make sure that they raise the money they need within their own deadlines? There are no specific answers to these questions. It is much a matter of your temperament and style as anthing else. But the following points might be helpful in improving your grantsmanship skills.

1. Apply immediately

Smaller applications for small sums to the smaller trusts can be sent out whenever you like. Many of these smaller trusts meet infrequently (often only once a year), and it may be some time before you hear the outcome of your appeal. So the sooner you get these applications out, the better.

2. The blanket approach

Suppose you have identified 50 trusts as being potentially interested in your work, you might then send out all 50 applications at once. The advantage of doing this is that you will have actually asked 50 trusts to support you; and they then have to decide whether to do so or not. The disadvantage is that your appeal may not be as strong as where you adopt the step-by-step approach *(discussed below)*. In your application you might state that you are approaching a number of trusts, including... *(giving the names of several trusts you are approaching)*. And you might try to indicate in some way how much you would like each trust to give. There are several techniques for doing this:

Ask directly for a specific sum *(£7,500, or £5,000 for 3 years)*.

State that you need to raise a specific sum which you hope to get from a specific number of trusts *(£20,000 from 6 trusts)* which gives a picture for how much each trust might contribute.

Provide a shopping list *(£12,000 for the project itself, £3,000 for the research, £3,000 for the publication, £2,000 for the evaluation)*.

If you have already received grants, then state how much has been committed and from what sources. This gives them the opportunity to peg their giving accordingly.

Most trusts will not reply. Some will acknowledge receipt of your application, and that will be the last you will hear. Some will want further information. A very few might request a meeting. Some will simply send you a cheque, if your application is successful.

You can use their reponse to improve your chances. If one of your top prospects says no, it may be worth finding out why, possibly asking for a meeting or a visit so that you can explain the importance of your work in greater depth. There are many instances of an applicant being able to turn a 'no' into a 'yes' in this way. In any case, you will begin to accumulate information about their approach to grant-making which will improve your chances of success next time.

If you have been successful, you can send a follow up letter to some of the other trusts that have not yet reached a decision, outlining the progress of the appeal. This can remind them that your appeal is outstanding as well as give them further information which might enhance your chances. If you fall just short of your target you might also consider going back and asking a selected few of your supporters if there is the possibility of topping up their support with a further small grant.

3. The step-by-step approach

Here you identify from your list of potential trusts a very few which you believe are more likely to be interested in you and which have the resources to make a substantial grant. How you approach them will depend on how well you are known to them and whether they have supported you previously. You may be able to arrange a meeting to discuss your proposal; you may want to find out first about the grant cycle, when applications are due in and when they will be considered.

Do all you can to persuade these trusts to support you. Once you have got a grant from one, you can begin to aproach others. The first grant reduces your target, and provides an endorsement for what you are doing. This makes it more likely that other trusts will agree to support you.

Mention to each trust you approach something of your fund-raising strategy. Ask for support at a specific level and put this into the context of your overall fund-raising plans for the project. For the first trusts, tell them who else you are approaching; tell them that you intend to approach a number of other trusts once they have decided to back you, and that their 'lead' grant will encourage others to give to you.

4. The delayed approach

In most applications you ask for money. But there are other possibilities. You can send an outline of your proposals and ask for a meeting. This would only be worthwhile where you are already well known to the trust. Otherwise, trusts will normally prefer a full written proposal in the first instance. You can try to get them to visit you. Open days, launches and other events can provide suitable oppportunities for this. If you are organising a prestigious event, this can be a particularly appropriate time to ask trusts to visit you.

Some projects, such as City Farms, have a 'product' which is inherently attractive to donors, and they find that most of the people who visit eventually decide to give financial support. In such circumstances, the challenge is to find ways of getting them to visit you.

You can try to get yourself known in the trust world before you actually apply. This means meeting trust administrators at events and conferences, and making sure you introduce yourself. It means sending out your annual report (for information purposes only) to potential supporters. It means seeking and getting publicity in the media. It means building your trustee, patron or supporter base so that you create wider contacts for your organisation.

A further point to note is that it is extremely hard to obtain substantial support for a project when you have never received support before. This may mean presenting more modest needs now, and building on this over time.

What to do after the application

Mostly you will do nothing, except wait for a yes or a no. However, it is possible to chase up your letter with a phone call, to find out if it has arrived, when it will be considered, and whether they require any further information. This, at least, has the advantage of putting a human voice to a written application. But you do need to do this carefully. There is a danger of appearing to harass them, which they will resent.

When you do receive a positive reply, then say thank you immediately. Put the donor on a mailing list to receive information on your work (such as annual reports and copies of the publications you produce). Note any conditions of the grant that have to be met (terms for spending the money, reporting and audit requirements, etc.).

Keep a card index on file of your contacts. Add information from your refusals as well as your successes. They may give reasons for turning you down. Note these, as this can help you next time. Although what they say may be out of politeness rather than the bare truth. When you do reapply, remind them that you have applied before. Remember that the trusts that have supported you this time are quite likely to want to support you again (unless they have a specific policy of not doing so). You should consider when and how next to approach them.

WRITING A FUND-RAISING PROPOSAL

As trusts normally work on annual grant cycles, you may decide to go back for more support next year. The trusts that have turned you down are also potentially likely supporters. You have decided that they are likely to be interested. The only problem is that they have not yet come to the same decision! Unless they have told you that they are really not interested, then there is still hope, and persistence can pay.

A first application should be seen as the beginning, not the end, of the process. Success in raising money from trusts depends as much on building relationships as on writing a good application for a good project.

Thinking in project terms

Trusts like to back projects, that is, identifiable aspects of your work, rather than to put money into administration or overhead costs. The reason for this is that they will feel that their money is actually being put to work. There is a great deal of skill in how you present the work you plan to do, in devising projects which will be attractive to donors. Some of the points to bear in mind are:

Innovation: trusts have traditionally liked to pioneer new work and new approaches.

Current concerns: projects which will address current concerns in the field of social action are more likley to receive support. Last year it might have been the inner city, this year the needs of rural areas, and next year perhaps the needs of outlying estates around the big cities. Interests and fashions change, and it is as well to pick up on what is felt to be important now.

Achievements and outcomes: where something specific and measurable is to be achieved then this will be more attractive than simply stating that the money will be spent for a good purpose. In one of the examples given in the next section, an applicant is applying for £2,000 to train 5 volunteers to undertake alcohol counselling. This is specific, achievable and will have some impact – all qualities of an attractive project.

Cost-effectiveness: projects should appear good value for money. This does not mean that you should pare down the application to the absolute minimum. On the contrary, if the project is attractive, it will pay to try to raise more money for it, not less. By apportioning overhead costs, allowing for all items of expenditure costed on a realistic basis and including contingencies, you can increase your financial need. The skill then becomes how to demonstrate the impact and effectiveness of the work, rather than to emphasise how cheaply it can be done.

Leverage: projects which will have a seemingly great impact for the expenditure will be more attractive. Most donors want to achieve more with their money.

Scale of the project: the project should not be so immense that the donor can only make a small contribution towards it. Or if it is, then it should be presented in such a way that the donor feels that his contribution is specially important, that it is the missing piece of the jigsaw which will complete the whole picture

Remember, a project is only an aspect of your work, highlighted for fund-raising purposes. Devising projects that will prove attractive to grant-makers is one of the more important skills of being a successful fund-raiser.

How to write a good application, from the trust administrator's viewpoint

Each trust is different, views applications differently, and has different procedures for deciding which applications to support and which to reject. The following comments made by the adminstrators of the Carnegie, Chase, Gulbenkian, Goldsmiths and Wates charities for the previous edition of this book give a flavour of the attitude, approach and procedures of those who will be dealing with your application.

'We try to do our job conscientiously because we recognise that the great majority of our applicants deserve serious and responsible consideration, and I end up with an enormous admiration for most of the people writing to us.'

'Please remember that we are swamped with applications. On a purely statistical basis your chances of success are not more than 10 per cent. We are getting many more applications than ever before; so you really do have to do your homework to find out the sort of things we are interested in, if you are to stand any chance of getting a grant.'

'These are some of the criteria by which we judge applications:

The quality of the leader of the project and the people involved in it.

The practical outcome of the work.

The degree of pioneering.

The degree of community participation.

The chances of the project having wider application if it succeeds.

The clarity of the objectives and the practicability of achieving them.

The accounts of the organisation being in good order and the budget estimates satisfactory.

The prospect of the project attaining financial self-sufficiency or attracting a statutory source of funding when the grant period ends.'

'When we get an application I first judge it against our guidelines, and I will also take into account the presentation of the application, the financial side, and the calibre of the management. Having formed some general impression I may cross-check; I will do this if I am still doubtful, or maybe anyway. I will talk to the directors of some like-minded trusts, or I may consult the panel of professional advisers we have. Then I will look at the availability of funds under the notional allocations we have made; I should state that these allocations are not completely rigid, but more in the nature of guidelines; and in any case a project might very well fall within more than one category. Next I have to decide whether to visit the project. At this stage I will have decided that we are seriously interested in it. I find this extremely difficult, because I would never want to make a recommendation to the trustees without a visit to the project or an interview with the project leader, but equally if I go to see a project and then do not recommend it (for whatever reason), it can raise expectations and cause a great deal of disappointment. But often when I do visit projects, I find that I get a completely different impression both of the applicant and of the project from what I have gained from the written application.

Finally I make my recommendations to the trustees and the trustees decide what to support.'

'We arrive at the final decision by means of a question and answer process:

'Is the project something for which statutory funds are available?' Or 'Is this something which fits better another trust's purposes and policies?'

If the answer is 'Yes', we would always try to suggest alternative funding sources.

'Does it differ significantly from a project we have supported in the recent past?' A scheme which, however good, was quite similar to something that had come up quite recently would not necessarily be rejected, but could be deferred.

'Is the proposal pioneering in a significant way?' and 'If it is of benefit in a particular locality, will it also provide lessons and benefits for other places?'

'Is the project well conceived and thought out?' This is not exactly the same thing as the standard of presentation of the application. Often a good idea will not be well presented, and here we would try to assist the applicant, with a view to maximising the chances of attracting a grant.

'If the project is seminal, pioneering, and well thought out, are the people behind it capable also of carrying it out satisfactorily?' We want to be assured that they have the necessary skills to implement it.

'What are the arrangements for long-term funding?' We would want to be certain that we were not starting something which later would probably collapse for lack of long-term finance.

'Does the cost fall within our means; can we afford to make the grant?' If the answer is 'No', and the scheme really has passed all the other tests, then we would not turn it down for that reason. We would look for partners. In these days we are all short of money and trusts tend to share the cost of schemes.

At the end of that long, long haul, if the poor applicant has successfully negotiated all these hurdles, the answer may still be 'No, we are sorry, we cannot help'. This would be because we have more good projects than we can possibly help.'

'We are very unsophisticated in the way we deal with applications. We rely very much on third-party advice. We use outside organisations, central bodies, and experts who have given us good advice in the past.

We value very much seeing familiar names on your own notepaper, those of your own trustees or patrons, for the obvious reason that we feel that if so-and-so has put his name to this charity, then that is a good start. This does not mean that if we do not recognise any of the names you have no chance of success.'

'However inept or tatty an application is, someone has put time and effort into it (sometimes it is not as much time and effort as they ought to have put; nevertheless they have tried, and very often one must remember that they are people doing voluntary work or people not very experienced in fund-raising). So that you must look for the good idea, even though it may be rather buried. At any rate, every application should receive due consideration.'

'A trust can help applicants in ways other than making grants. We can refer them to other trusts, possibly doing some spadework first. Sometimes they really could borrow money, rather than have a grant; and I do not mean borrow it from trusts, but borrow it commercially; and this is where one can see that they can generate the income which will enable them to service the loan. Sometimes they do not know about statutory money that could be available to them.'

'We are really working in a kind of partnership with our clients or beneficiaries. We are trying to reach the same goal; we have two different functions in getting there, the one providing the money, the other doing the work. But ours is the easier; I always admire the people who are doing the work on the ground.'

'The only appeal letters we do not reply to are either unsigned or they are duplicated with a facsimile signature. Even then, if there is something interesting in it for us, we probably would reply. In these days of sophisticated office equipment, it is not always possible to tell whether or not it is a circular letter, if it is cunningly enough worded (but having three trusts I often receive the same personalised appeal to all of them).'

'Every application is listed, with a brief summary of what it is about and why I have turned it down, and this list goes to the trustees at every meeting. I feel the trustees have a right to know what appeals have come in, and clients have a right to expect that trustees do know.'

'A large proportion of the people who apply to us have never taken the trouble to find out the policies of the trust. This does not make a good beginning, for it is a waste of time, effort and money on everyone's part dealing with inappropriate applications and with general appeals.'

'In your approach to us, the opening paragraph should be the 'punch' paragraph which should set the scene and also gain the attention of the reader, grip the imagination, succinctly describe the key aspects of the project and command respect. This should be followed by a description of the structure of the scheme showing how an imaginative idea and the initiative of the promoter is buttressed by a sound management committee. The application should then proceed to establish in practical terms and without resorting to jargon the main aims of the scheme and how this fits into the organisation as a whole. Finally there should be a very concise summary. Perhaps an analogy to a four-course meal might be appropriate, but beware the sweet course; flattery will get you nowhere, but courtesy and sheer delight may bring you satisfaction. With your letter of application – two pages should really be more than sufficient to express the main aims of your scheme and how you intend to undertake it – you can attach as appendices your budget, your annual accounts, details of your organisation, its objects, membership and committee structure. From our point of view, if you get it right first time, you are either brilliant or lucky; but you must show an understanding of your project and of the trust's policies, if your application is to go any further.'

'I like to deal with the leader of the project or the director of the organisation. We never liaise with professional consultants or fund-raising staff because we do not respond to general appeals. This does not mean that applications from fund-raisers are consigned to the waste-paper basket, but in the follow up I want to be able to discuss the project with those who will be responsible for running it.'

'Why do we reject? We are unable to get a quart out of a pint pot; that is the main problem.'

WRITING A BETTER APPLICATION: SOME WORKED EXAMPLES

In the following pages we reproduce some actual appeal letters sent out by smaller organisations to see how they can be improved. We have disguised the actual applicants to save embarassment! These examples put some of the 'theory' expounded in the previous pages into a practical context, and show how some quite simple changes can help improve your chances of success significantly.

Example 1

Dear ...,

Eastern Trust is a charity working in ... with young people who are experiencing social and emotional problems, caused by the stress of living in the disadvantaged areas of the county.

For 28 years, Eastern Trust has offered potentially delinquent children an opportunity to invest their energies in more constructive activities than vandalism, glue-sniffing and other forms of anti-social behaviour. At a time when there is great national concern about symptoms like vandalism, violence and truancy, and when Social Service budgets are being reduced, the approach is particularly apt. It falls within the general spirit of Intermediate Treatment and can also be used as an adjunct to care and supervision. The Trust uses the small group approach (2 volunteer leaders to 8 children) and organises activities on a weekly basis, with occasional residential week-ends and an annual holiday for each group.

In general, the children are referred from statutory services as being likely to experience difficulties, and present society not only with problems, but also with high cost (i.e. Social Service and Court costs).

WRITING A BETTER APPLICATION

At the moment the Trust has two paid staff, a project co-ordinator and an administrator, whose salaries are funded by Urban Aid. It has had a second project co-ordinator seconded from the County Youth and Community Department, but this support has been withdrawn.

Urban Aid funding ceases next March, and we are urgently seeking help to continue the work of Eastern Trust with children in the area. May we please come to see you to talk about this.

Yours sincerely,

J.W. Director

1. Making a good case

This application is from a small local charity working with young people at risk and using volunteers. The key points it needs to highlight in the application are:

The importance of the problem, and that something can be done about it.

The method of working using volunteers. This is something that some donors will find attractive.

The partnership with the statutory sector with referrals coming from social services, etc. Projects which complement and supplement existing provision are also attractive.

The ability of the trust to do a good job cost-effectively, based on its track record of achievement.

Some of these points are made, but they could be made rather more forcefully.

2. Be specific, not general

The application is rather general, and could certainly be improved by giving information on the success rate of the trust's work.

Evaluation of the work: Has any evaluation or follow up been done? If not, perhaps this needs thinking about.

Facts and figures on the problem: the county is in one of the more disadvantaged regions of the country, and the trust works in a disadvantaged part of the county. Can this be expressed factually (e.g. in statistics on truancy, street crime, vandalism, relative to the natural average)?

Facts and figures on the achievements of the organisation: how many children are seen each year, how many volunteers, how many events and activities in a typical week.

Credibility: All apart from some local funding bodies will know little or nothing of the work being done by the trust. Is there any way in which the trust can show itself in a good light – patrons, commendations, press reports, etc.?

3. The funding context

The main problem of this application is in fact not how it is written, but the long-term funding position of the trust. It has had an equivalent of three staff through the County Council (via a secondment and the Urban Programme). With overhead costs, this must be worth at least £30,000 a year. But the secondment has been withdrawn and Urban Programme support becomes time-expired from next March. Has the trust got a future? Who is going to pay the staff? If money is raised, can it continue to be raised on an on-going basis? The running costs of the project will have to be paid not just next year, but the year after and the year after that... Is there any realistic probablity of statutory funding being continued:

By the Urban Programme grant being extended, or replaced by a direct grant from the local authority.

Through some other programme – for example Opportunities for Volunteering which pays the costs of co-ordinating unemployed and other volunteers for social service projects, or the Safer Cities Programme run by the Home Office. Programme hopping from one statutory programme to another has been one method of survival for many local projects. By a mixture of support from different sources, such as the youth service, the police community fund, social services, etc. It is often possible to piece together the running costs of the organisation in this way.

Failing this, what can be done? It is almost certainly unrealistic to plan for an organisation employing three staff to exist without any form of statutory support or other long-term income. Money from trusts and other sources will only be given to organisations which demonstrate an ability to stay in business. The bulk of the core costs need to be secured first, before approaching trusts. If this proves impossible, then it might be possible to run the organisation in a different way – for example, using volunteers to help in the administration and the training, supported by just one project organiser working part-time. A low-cost contingency plan such as this could be fundable.

Before applying to anyone, it is important for any organisation to sort out what statutory funding is obtainable, and to devise a realistic and achievable funding strategy for the future. Once this has been done, and only then, can outside funding bodies, such as trusts, be approached to provide incidental or supplementary expenditure for equipment, visits, activities, or to pay for new initiatives or developments.

4. The request

This application asks for a meeting to discuss the possibility of funding, rather than asking for money. More often you will want to ask for a grant or donation right away. In such circumstances, it is best to decide how much you want the donor to give, and ask for a specific amount. Too many applications, having made a good case for support, tail off at the end by mumbling about making a generous contribution to our appeal. What is generous? How much should they give? By leaving it to them, they are being asked to make *two* decisions – whether to support you *and* how much to give. A cardinal rule of fund-raising is to make it as easy as possible for the donor to say yes. You can do this by leaving them with only one decision to make to your specific proposal (a yes or a no).

Example 2

Dear........,

The misuse of alcohol plays a part in many health, emotional and social problems. These may include accidents on the road, at home and at work; family problems may include violence, poverty and divorce; crimes of vandalism, violence and drink driving; health problems such as liver damage, brain damage and gastritis; personal problems of depression, guilt and loneliness. Knowing what to do is not always easy.

The Alcohol Counselling Service is a registered charity and voluntary organisation established in 1981. We offer Counselling, Training, Education and Information on Alcohol. We provide a private and confidential service to the community free of charge, with trained voluntary counsellors who give their time freely and who see up to 50 people every week whose lives have been affected directly or indirectly by alcohol misuse. We have already helped and advised thousands of people in ... who came to us with very personal and private problems. Without our service to the people of ..., the problems associated with alcohol will continue.

WRITING A BETTER APPLICATION

Will you help us to continue to provide this essential service to the community by contributing towards a project designed to provide approximately five trained voluntary counsellors to work with people who have alcohol related problems and who will also support their families. The anticipated cost of the project is £2,000. I enclose a programme of working and costing.

I hope that you will be able to give favourable consideration to our request for support. If you would like to discuss this initiative further or require more information, please contact me.

Yours sincerely,

M.D., Director

This is a very similar application to *Example 1*. It meets many of the points made about that application. It is much more specific: 50 people a week are helped. A sum of £2,000 is asked for to pay for the training of 5 counsellors. A donor could decide to give the whole amount or to pay for the training of one or more counsellors at £400 per trainee. It also has the merit of being brief and to the point.

Three points could be made more strongly by providing examples to illustrate the point that is being made:

The problem: The organisation is helping people whose lives have been affected directly or indirectly by alcohol misuse. It is possible to give some examples of specific cases. It may also be possible to provide some relevant statistics about the extent of the problem in the region and nationally.

The success rate: Are there any statistics available on the success rate of providing a counselling service?

Cost-effectiveness: Using volunteers is often perceived as a very cost-effective way of dealing with a problem. They are giving their time free. The donor is being asked to pay for training or co-ordination, which is really an investment in the project. For the £2,000 that it will cost to train 5 counsellors, how many volunteer hours will this create in counsellor time, and how much would this be worth if the volunteers were paid (say £3 to £4 per hour) for their time? By providing this sort of rough calculation, you can demonstrate that the donor will be buying £10,000 or £20,000 of output for the investment in training. This 'leverage' makes the proposition that much more attractive. Another approach is to examine the outcome. By sorting out people's alcohol problems, how much is being saved by society. Here it may only be possible to guess at the figures. But even then, this does provide some idea of the effectiveness of the project.

Example 3

Dear......,

I write on behalf of the above project to ask if ... Fund could help us with a grant.

Our project is to encourage good neighbourliness and to develop a care network for elderly, lonely and especially housebound people within the area. At present we have 100 elderly and housebound tuned in to the network and volunteers keep a regular eye on them. This is only a very small proportion of the population, as at the last census it was revealed that this area has a higher percentage of elderly than the county average.

During the summer we should like to take these people on an outing. However, for many of them to climb into an ordinary coach would be out of the question. Therefore, we must hire one with a tail lift that can accommodate wheelchairs. This reduces the number that can be carried in a vehicle, eg: a 39-seater that takes 4 wheelchairs on board can only take 25 people.

To take these people out for a day we estimate that it will cost approximately £385 for transport alone, without giving them any refreshments. Raising funds in our neighbourhood is very difficult as there is high unemployment in the area. We should be very grateful for whatever the committee feels would be appropriate.

Yours faithfully,

A.S. Community Project Worker

Many smaller projects have quite modest financial needs. Here is a simple request to a smaller trust which makes small grants for local purposes. A good clear case is made. The application is factual and the organisation is made to appear competent. Here are several suggestions for enhancing the proposal:

1. Stress the achievements of the organisation
From this letter we know that the organisation serves a network of 100 elderly people and is about to take some of them on an outing.

Most readers of the application will know little or nothing about the organisation. So anything else you can tell them about what it does and its achievements and successes can only be helpful.

2. Community involvement
How many people are involved as volunteers? How much is raised from the local community? If, for example, some of the costs of the outing were met from local fund-raising, that would make the proposal seem that much more attractive.

3. Don't apologise
The application states that the organisation only helps a very small proportion of the elderly population. It is already helping 100 people, which is a real achievement. The fact that there is a lot more to do is a challenge. How to set about doing this and what financial resources would be required would be the subject for a further proposal. The fact that the organisation is planning to tackle the problem of unmet needs in the community is a positive statement, which is better than making a negative statement that the organisation is not doing enough.

Example 4

Dear ......,

I am writing to you to request financial support from your trust to help us at the Centre effectively continue our important work in the town.

The Centre was set up as a direct response to the lack of facilities for unwaged/unemployed people in the town, which has a particularly high level of unemployment presently standing at 18 per cent. We started as a small group running classes in rooms within council premises, and have grown to provide a large variety of courses and facilities within our building, which we rent from the County Council. Now, with sufficient space at our disposal, we are also able to support the work of many other community, self-help and charitable groups in the area by the provision of rooms for activities and meetings.

The Centre is different from many other organisations that do similar work. This is because it was set up to respond to a need by those who actually had that need: the unwaged, who therefore have a very stong influence in the running and policy of the Centre. We feel that this has assisted us to effectively provide a whole variety of opportunities to learn and practise new skills, and has helped the organisation not to lose touch with those it set out to help.

However, even with the use of volunteer tutors and general helpers, a core of paid staff are essential to provide continuity and support for the high level of activity that goes on in the Centre and for the development of new ideas.

Within our playcentre, staff are also required to enable us to register with Social Services and therefore operate within the law. A particularly high level of skill and understanding is needed in this sensitive area and therefore we feel it particularly important to have the continuity of qualified staff to maintain the high level of confidence needed in the provision of this service, that is so vital to maintain free access to the Centre.

Although some staff are paid through our Inner Area Programme grant until 1990, we need an administrative worker and two full-time equivalent creche staff to maintain the effective access to, and running of, our Centre's facilities. We are also worried that if we were unable to provide these workers, and activities were in decline leading up to April 1990, it would severely affect our attempts to secure the Centre's future beyond then.

It is for these reasons we are asking you for £... to pay for ... from ... to ... *(these blanks are filled in with different amounts/information depending on the source being approached).* This is only a small portion of our overall requirement which is detailed in the enclosures, but we feel that it is only fair and sensible to try and spread the necessary financial support as widely as possible. Therefore, we are applying to a number of trusts for the support we need.

We hope you will realise the value and importance of the work we have undertaken in this particularly needy area, and find yourselves in a position to help us. Please read the enclosures which will give you more details of the areas of our work, along with the philosophies and structure that underlie it.

If you wish to visit the Centre or require any further information, please do not hesitate to contact me.

Yours sincerely,

C.H. Co-ordinating Manager

WRITING A BETTER APPLICATION

Enclosures:
'The Case for Support' – A brief description of the work of the Centre and its need for support at the present time.
Constitution
Publicity Material
Annual Report
Timetable.

Budget for Support Services from: January 1989 – April 1990
Please note all figures include employer's costs.

Administration	
One full-time worker (Jan 1989 – March 1989)	£2,330.00
One full-time worker (April 1989 – March 1990)	£7,000.00
Total	**£9,330.00**
Creche	
One full-time Assistant Creche Organiser (Jan 1989 – March 1989)	£2,330.00
Two Part-time Play Leaders (Jan 1989 – March 1989)	£2,660.00
Total	**£4,990.00**
One full-time Assistant Creche Organiser (April 1989 – March 1990)	£7,000.00
Two part-time Play Leaders (April 1989 – March 1990)	£8,000.00
Total	**£15,000.00**
Total amount required	**£29,320.00**

This is a more ambitious application for a larger organisation. The organisation happens to enjoy a particularly high reputation locally. Like many receiving statutory grants, its core funding is not secure. In this instance the IAP (Urban Programme) grant runs until 1990 (eighteen months from the date of the application). Even so, the organisation still requires two full-time and two part-time workers to be paid for out of this application.

This proposal differs from *Example 1* because the organisation is more substantial. It has a large building and a wide range of activities. It has a wide spectrum of supporters and is thinking about the future (all this is outlined in *The case for support* which accompanied the application). For these reasons it should be more optimistic about its future, however uncertain the present sources of funding are.

The request is for support for 15 months. But what is going to happen in April 1990 when the IAP grant and the support received via this application both run out? Why not ask for longer-term support, say for 2 or 3 years. Trust grants do not have to run concurrently with the local authority year.

By asking for longer-term support at least all the grants will not run out at the same time. Some attempt should be made to identify the possible substantial sources of funding which will allow the organisation to continue beyond 1990, and the likelihood of obtaining a mixture of statutory sources, and a major grant from a trust or trusts. Other points which can enhance the application all relate to credibility building. More facts and figures on the neighbourhood in which the Centre operates. More information on its activities and services. More information on those statutory bodies, trusts and companies that have given the Centre support. If the application is going to be sent to trusts who are not familiar with the area, it is important to provide enough information to show that the Centre is a major, successful and important local project, and that this is more than *just another application.*

The final point is how to set about the asking. Do you circulate the appeal to a large number of trusts? Do you pick one or two major trusts first? Do you send a letter, or try to discuss your proposals in person? For an established project such as this, it is probably best to try to secure one large grant first, as it will make the remainder of the fund-raising that much easier. There will be less to raise, and the support of a major funder will entice others. In the region where this applicant operates, there is one major trust. The first objective should be to secure a grant from this trust (which did in fact support the project). The trust administrator could also advise on other larger trusts likely to be interested in supporting the project, and even intervene on the Centre's behalf.

Part 3

CASE STUDIES

THE CADBURY TRUSTS

The Barrow and Geraldine S Cadbury Trust, the Paul S Cadbury Trust and the Barrow Cadbury Fund Ltd.

1. History and Background

The Barrow and Geraldine S Cadbury Trust, the Paul S Cadbury Trust and the Barrow Cadbury Fund were all founded between the two world wars. They make grants for differing purposes but share the same general grant-making criteria as well as a common ethos. The Trusts were established as vehicles for the personal charitable concerns of their respective founders, and although none of them are alive now, the Trusts are basically still controlled by members of the Cadbury family. When Paul Cadbury died quite recently in 1984, the trustees declared the broad purpose of the reconstituted Paul S Cadbury Trust to be 'the fostering of people's self-confidence, voice and influence, knowledge and skills, and feelings of involvement and well-being'. This translates in practical terms to the encouragement of democratic forms at a local level.

The Barrow Cadbury Fund was originally set up in 1924 as a benevolent fund, but in 1949 it registered as a benevolent company. It does not have charitable status and is largely used to make grants whose purpose falls within the same areas of interest as the two Trusts, but which are not deemed to be charitable under the law.

There are a number of other 'Cadbury Trusts', but these are entirely separate from the three considered here which are administered together.

2. Objects and Policy

The Trusts make grants either to local projects based in the West Midlands, or to projects of national significance. More specifically, the policies of the Barrow and Geraldine S Cadbury Trust can be summarised as follows:

The support of fuller employment, through training and community business development;

The promotion of equal opportunities and racial justice, especially through black-led projects;

Penal affairs: support for victims of crime and the rehabilitation of offenders, including mediation schemes;

Small grants for better housing and community services;

Backing for initiatives promoting arms control and international peace.

The smaller Paul S Cadbury Trust supports the development of, and research into, local community organisations, emphasizing both individual and group participation in neighbourhood issues. It also supports some community arts projects and has a small grant-making programme in Northern Ireland fostering communication and co-operation across sectarian divisions.

The Barrow Cadbury Fund makes grants for non-charitable work in the fields covered by the two Trusts.

3. Grant Guidelines

The Trusts and Fund have an annual grant budget totalling over £1.4 million (1989), about seventy per cent of which is held by the Barrow and Geraldine S Cadbury Trust. The largest categories of expenditure are peace and international relations, race relations and equal opportunities, and employment.

The trustees approach to international relations is informed by a strong Quaker tradition and the belief 'that world peace – and, indeed, survival – is basically a political question, not an issue which can be left to the technologies of the market place'. They supported, for example, the Alternative Defence Commission, which attempted to specify the link between a non-threatening national defence policy and the political resolution of conflict both in Europe and globally. Anthony Wilson, Secretary of the larger Trust and the Fund, points out that a policy of promoting local and international reconciliation and social justice does not necessarily imply neutrality: 'Where human rights are the issue....a *split the difference* approach would have scant regard to the justice element.'

Work on race relations and equal opportunities has moved from earlier support for a multi-racial input for voluntary projects to targeting initiatives actively promoting equal opportunities and fighting discrimination. Some of this activity (as in all the areas of Trust support) is not legally classified as 'charitable'; the Barrow Cadbury Fund has been used to make grants to the Campaign Against Racist Laws and the West Midlands Divided Family Campaign, among others.

The Barrow and Geraldine S Cadbury Trust emphasizes that its work on employment has had 'less to do with *tea and sympathy* than with provision of training and child-care resources that can release people for employment.' This includes the development of infrastructural support: making grants to give small, local businesses access to sector-specific training and technology. The Trust maintains an uneasy dialogue with government policy – encouraging entrepreneurial initiative but criticising, for example, the restrictive nature of the new Employment Training Scheme. It is also uncomfortably aware that its limited resources can only mitigate the worst effects of under-employment and has supported groups which 'engage in constructive if critical dialogue with decision-makers whose policies rate countering inflation as a higher priority than deliberately creating jobs'.

The trustees do not often give one-off grants, and increasingly are looking to make grants larger, fewer in number, and probably over a longer period. This means that most of the income is already tied up at the beginning of each year. Most grants are for specific projects, where trustees operate what is described as a 'counter-Stock Exchange' approach. This does not mean that the Trusts will support losers, just that 'We set a high premium on the fact that the applicant isn't likely to get the money from anywhere else....If we think that an application is *appeal-worthy*, that is, that it could get funds from another source, we are not likely to back it'.

The Cadbury Trusts, then, rarely respond to general appeals and are even more emphatic than most trusts about keeping within their policy guidelines and discouraging inappropriate applications. As Anthony Wilson has put it: 'We're terribly sorry; we love whales too; but we just don't do whales'.

4. Trustees

The trustees of the Barrow and Geraldine S Cadbury Trust, who are also the Directors of the Barrow Cadbury Fund, are listed below. Those marked with an asterisk are in addition trustees of the Paul S Cadbury Trust.

Full trustees' meetings are usually held four times a year.

5. Staff

Anthony Wilson is the Secretary to the Barrow and Geraldine S Cadbury Trust and the Barrow Cadbury Fund, with Joe Montgomery as Assistant Secretary. Eric Adams is Secretary to the Paul S Cadbury Trust and Deputy Secretary to the other Trust and the Fund.

6. Grant procedure and advice to applicants

Rather than have an application form, Trust staff prefer to see copies of minutes and working papers with an application and will usually discuss with the applicant as to how these relate to the Trusts' concerns. The size of a potential grant would also come under discussion: whether, for example, it would be better if part of the funding came from a different source. It is hoped that a relationship of trust can thus be built up before any grant is made.

The Trusts' commitment to promoting equal opportunities goes beyond the grants made in that specific category. Most of the work is aimed towards promoting a more equitable distribution of social goods, and any applicant for Trust support is expected to take the necessary steps to ensure that their project is open to participation by people of any race or sex, whether as committee members, members of staff, volunteers, or beneficiaries/clientele.

7. Issues

'When we make a grant it is a statement of our commitment to that agency's work....So we expect there to be a very considerable after-sales service.' The Trusts frequently draw attention to the fact that they do more than just sign cheques, and with the concentration of their grant-making on fewer projects comes a greater emphasis on monitoring and assessment. After-sales service can in fact include anything from general advice to paying to have a grant-recipient's accounts professionally audited. The Trusts' pro-active tendency is currently demonstrated in the promotion of a citizen organisation which it is hoped will lead to the creation of a UK Citizen Organising Foundation, and in the launch of the Loans Guarantee Consortium as an independent company. The Consortium guarantees bank loans for those starting their own businesses, many of whom are from sections of the community which are often not deemed credit-worthy by bank managers.

On a wider scale, the trustees' commitment to the entire project of their grant-making extends from the ethical investment of Trust assets, including the compilation of a 'miss-list' of named companies, to the continual revision and evaluation of their grant-making strategy: 'With the limited resources available to them trustees must seek out the margins at which contributions can be effective'. The desire for greater national co-ordination between grant-makers is perhaps a natural continuation of this concern with strategy, and trustees are looking hopefully to the development of the UK Association of Charitable Foundations.

THE CARNEGIE UNITED KINGDOM TRUST

1. History and Background

The Carnegie UK Trust dates from 1913, when it was founded with an endowment of $10 million in US Steel Corporation bonds. Its assets now have a market value of about £16 million. The founder was Andrew Carnegie, a Scotsman who made his fortune in the US steel industry and used it to create a multi-national charitable empire. One of his first and most celebrated ventures was the establishment and funding of public libraries, and over 80% of his fortune (some $350 million) was used for educational purposes of one form or other, whether for libraries, universities and colleges, or research institutions.

The trustees of the United Kingdom Trust still qualify their policies with the idea of informal and popular education, but Carnegie's foresight was to leave the Trust Deed sufficiently non-specific to accomodate changes in social conditions over the three-quarters of a century since the Trust's foundation. Its stated object was 'the improvement of the well-being of the masses of the people of Great Britain and Ireland, by such means as are embraced within the meaning of the word charitable according to Scottish or English law, and which the trustees might from time to time select as best fitted from age to age for securing these purposes, remembering that new needs are constantly arising as the masses advance'. Policies are developed by the trustees in five-year periods, but there is a large degree of continuity from one quinquennial policy to the next.

THE CARNEGIE UNITED KINGDOM TRUST

2. Objects and policy

In the current quinquennium, 1986–1990, applications are considered under the following three headings:

1. Amateur Arts: the concentration is on the encouragement of amateur participation in the arts, particularly linking the arts with the local community and environment. This includes the development of local festivals, community drama and amateur/professional co-operation. There is also an emphasis on arts and disabled people, with support for a new national ADAPT Fund for improving accessibility to arts venues.

2. The Environment: support for small-scale, practical projects to conserve or improve the local environment, particularly involving voluntary participation; planning for urban wildlife schemes; environmental education and heritage interpretation.

3. Community Service: schemes prioritised in this category are those concerned with family care and parenting, the involvement of the young unemployed or those at risk, and the recently retired. Once again the emphasis is on local involvement, voluntary action and leadership.

Within each of the main categories above there are in addition two areas of special consideration, as follows:

Independent Learning: support for voluntary organisations for up to 75 per cent grant aid towards new informal learning opportunities of a non-residential nature.

New Technology: grants towards the cost of new office technology for voluntary organisations with which the Trust has a special link.

3. Grant Guidelines

Each of the three categories has received roughly the same in grants during this quinquennial period, with Amateur Arts so far receiving slightly more. 78 grants were approved in 1988, worth a total of £782,000.

The Trust often works in association with umbrella groups to provide national allocation schemes which benefit local groups, for example with the Civic Trust, the Pre-school Playgroups Association, the British Federation of Music Festivals and the National Federation of Community Organisations. It will sometimes liaise with other trusts and funding agencies to raise the support required for a particular venture.

Grants are made to charitable organisations in the UK and the Irish Republic *for charitable purposes only*. Priority is given to national organisations, but only where the work benefits 'local grass roots action'. Grants are only given to local group schemes when they display innovation and are likely to be of national significance.

There are numerous exclusions. These include areas of work supported in the past by the Trust but not covered by the current quinquennial policy. In addition, grants are not made for:

Personal study, travel, or expeditions;

Formal education;

Medical or related purposes;

Animal welfare;

Research or publications.

The Trust never responds to general appeals or provides grants for the general funds of an organisation, for endowment funds, for closed societies or to relieve statutory bodies of their responsibility.

Since 1982 the Trust has also administered the Unemployed Voluntary Action Fund, funded by the Scottish Office, for voluntary initiatives in Scotland involving the unemployed. In 1989/90 grant-in-aid was £627,000.

4. Trustees

There are twenty-two life trustees, of whom eighteen sit on the Executive Committee. The Chair is Mrs Catherine C Sharp MBE JP BCom, with Anthony Mould JP as Vice-Chair.

There is a sub-committee for each of the main areas of policy. Lady Wagner (Governor at the National Institute for Social Work and Chair of the Volunteer Centre) is Convenor for the Community Service sub-committee, David Tudway Quilter for Amateur Arts and William Thomson for the Environment.

5. Staff

The Secretary and Treasurer of the Trust is Geoffrey Lord, a former

Deputy-Chief Probation Officer. Elizabeth East is the Administrative Assistant, and there are seven other staff.

6. Grant Procedures and Advice to Applicants

The Carnegie UK Trust is unusually specific in its grants policy, which is outlined above but is described in considerably greater detail in its Quinquennial Policy leaflet, available from the Trust. Intending applicants are advised to read this, as well as the Trust's Annual Report which should be available in any main public library. It is worth noting that the majority of applications received by the Trust actually fall outside the area of interest of its work, and it no longer replies to every unsolicited application. 'Duplicated type appeals sent indiscriminately to all and sundry will not be acknowledged.'

Written applications should be addressed to the Secretary of the Trust and can be submitted at any time, although preferably at an early planning stage. The trustees look for flair and innovation, evidence of sound planning, support of a good committee structure, and community participation. The present Secretary, Geoffrey Lord, suggests a two to three page letter of application with your organisation's budget, annual accounts, objects and structure attached as appendices. He writes: 'In your approach to us, the opening paragraph should be the punch paragraph which should set the scene and also gain the attention of the reader, grip the imagination, succinctly describe the key aspects of the project and command respect'. If this sounds a tall order, don't panic. 'Practically no applications we receive are suitable in their original form....if you get it right the first time you are either brilliant or lucky'. In actual fact, applications will usually be developed in correspondence with the trust, and it is hoped that the process will provide a degree of constructive criticism and support.

Promising project applications are discussed with the Convenor of the appropriate sub-committee so there is input at an early stage from someone with knowledge and experience in the field. The trust, incidently, won't liaise with fund-raising staff or consultants but prefers 'to discuss the project with those who will be responsible for running it'.

7. Issues

A recent annual report characterizes the development of a new quinquennial policy as evolution rather than revolution. The Trust points out that it 'can only accept for consideration those applications that happen to come to it, but part of its work is to seek out rewarding areas of interest, and bring together on neutral ground people with ideas from different disciplines and from the ensuing discussions distil the essence of new thoughts for new policies'. So far the distillation process has produced the following pointers for 1991–1995:

Life, Work and Livelihood in the Third Age: occupation in retirement for those over 55 years of age and a consideration of the wider implications for this age group of current demographic changes and changes in service provision and the labour market;

The support of voluntary **self-help groups**; also of voluntary home-visiting services for families undergoing stress, carers for the elderly, and retired and senior volunteers;

Support for the development of a form of **nationwide community service**;

A limited scheme for assisting **village halls**;

Improved training in **environmental interpretation, education and conservation**.

It should be stressed that these are potential areas of interest for the Trust and do not constitute policy (as yet).

On a more general note, the trustees see their role as innovatory, and although they won't give long-term revenue support they will 'try to assist....over a reasonable length of time in the initial stages of important new developments'.

THE GULBENKIAN FOUNDATION

1. History and Background

The Calouste Gulbenkian Foundation is an international grant-making body based in Lisbon, Portugal, where its headquarters form an arts complex comprising a museum, libraries, concert-halls, a pavilion, theatres (indoor and open air), galleries, exhibition and conference facilities, and a scientific research centre. The Foundation's UK Branch, based in London, occupies rather more modest offices in the north east corner of Portland Place and makes grants in the United Kingdom and the Irish Republic. Its not inconsiderable grants budget approached £1.5 million in 1988.

The Foundation is named after Calouste Sarkis Gulbenkian, an Armenian born in Istanbul in 1869. Gulbenkian pursued a commercial and industrial career, mainly in oil. He worked in Britain, becoming a British citizen and a Fellow of King's College, London, but finally settled in Portugal where he died in 1955, a year before the Foundation – now Europe's largest – was established.

2. Objects and Policy

The UK Branch of the Foundation administers grants in the following five programmes:

1. Arts: mainly public visual arts projects, ethnic minority arts, the development and training of experienced artists, and training opportunities in the UK involving contact with foreign influences.

2. Education: mainly arts projects for young people, educational innovations and developments.

3. Social Welfare: mainly neighbourhood work initiatives, neighbourhood care and self-help schemes, and the development of support services for local groups.

4. Republic of Ireland: hitherto encouraging public involvement in the conservation and appreciation of Irish heritage, and support for Arts in the Community and Education (ACE); now more generally, but within a limited total budget of £100,000 p.a.

5. Anglo-Portuguese Cultural Relations: activities in the UK and Ireland to do with Portugal, cultural and educational interaction between the countries, and the needs of Portuguese immigrant communities.

3. Grant Guidelines

Considering the Foundation's size, grants made are quite small, generally under £7,000, with a notional limit of £15,000. Although individuals are occasionally supported, most of the recipients are registered charities. The Foundation will usually deal with the headquarters rather than the local branches of an organisation, favouring 'projects of more than local significance'. Small, local projects are aided perhaps more constructively in the Social Welfare programme through backing the development of the voluntary sector infrastructure: information, training and back-up services.

The Gulbenkian Foundation stresses the importance of encouraging innovation. The Director of the Arts programme, Iain Reid, explains: 'If the arts are to develop and survive then artists doing more daring work, which may well be obscure, risky or disturbing, must also receive support'. More generally, a preference is given to 'new developments, not yet a part of the regular running costs of an organisation; and to developments regarded either as strategic, because they provide facilities in a geographical area notably deficient in them, or as seminal, because they seem likely to influence policy and practice elsewhere'. Among new projects initiated by the Foundation itself there have been a series of open award schemes, including in the past a Community Arts Apprentice Scheme, a Large Scale Events Scheme and a Documentary Arts Award Scheme for schools.

The Foundation's 'Guiding Principles', published in its leaflet 'Advice to applicants for grants' (sent on request), consist almost entirely of a near-exhaustive list of negatives. Areas not supported include: science and medicine, alcohol and drug abuse, the elderly, individual education and training, and grants will not be made for building costs, travel, to pay off debts or to make up withdrawn statutory funding.

4. Trustees

The Gulbenkian Foundation has a Board which meets in Lisbon and to which the UK Branch is responsible through its member in Britain.

5. Staff

The Foundation's UK Director is Ben Whitaker, previously Executive Director of the Minority Rights Group, former Junior Minister and Labour MP for Hampstead and author of 'The Foundations'. The other senior staff are:

Paul Curno, Deputy Director and in charge of Social Welfare

Iain Reid, Assistant Director, Arts (who will be leaving at the end of 1989)

Simon Richey, Assistant Director, Education

Millicent Bowerman, Literary Editor and Librarian.

6. Grant procedure and advice to applicants

The Foundation's printed leaflet sets out detailed criteria for each of its funding programmes, but Ben Whitaker hints at a certain scope for flexibility: 'Parts of its text can be overtaken by new ideas and arguments of sufficient merit – which I hope we will always receive'. If in doubt, start by sending off a brief outline of what you intend, and a member of staff will advise.

There is no recommended format for applications, but there is a checklist of essential information, as follows: the exact purpose for which funding is sought, itemised details of the amount required and the total budget, information on other sources of income (both secure and potential), the legal and tax status of your organisation, and its function. This last condition is best satisfied by providing a copy of the organisation's constitution, or, if established, its latest annual report and accounts.

As it has no board of trustees in the UK, the Foundation has to rely on a stream of outside consultants and specialist contacts. The handling of a proposal – which might include such consultation, discussion with the applicant, possible modification of the project, and perhaps an on-site visit – usually takes some time.

7. Issues

At a time when the statutory sector seems unlikely to assume new responsibilities, many trusts and foundations are re-thinking what has for so long been considered their most specific function: 'pump-priming'. Not so the Gulbenkian, where emphasis on initial funding for the 'seminal' project remains undiminished. Ben Whitaker argues, 'At present the situation is in danger of becoming exactly the reverse: foundations risk losing their freedom to originate if they devote their limited budgets to picking up the casualties from the public sector....Acquiesence in such requests will all too likely compound the future problem'. After all, foundations were never in the business of providing, or even helping to provide, a universal service, and 'it is less than logical to deduce from not being able to help all one-legged dogs that one should not help any one-legged dog'. A popular interim solution is to lengthen the period of initial funding for new projects, and back in 1981 Richard Mills, a consultant to the Foundation, recognized 'the need to sustain for a while longer a good scheme for which alternative long-term funding is not yet in sight'. But it seems that this has not been adopted on any systematic basis, and Ben Whitaker now confirms, 'Because of our economic constraints it is rare for us to be able to finance a project, however excellent, more than once'.

The Gulbenkian Foundation is, however, keen to co-fund projects with other funding agencies. It is also anxious to co-operate with other trusts in working out the problems trusts face in developing their role for the future, and has helped play a part in organising Trust Administrators' Groups on particular issues. New areas of interest it is presently considering for its own work include the meanings and implications of 'active citizenship'; inner city problems, including alienated youth, vandalism and graffiti; rural disadvantage; bullying in schools; projects on women's problems; and priorities for helping in the Republic of Ireland. Another of the Foundation's interests, and one it shares with several other trusts, is project monitoring and evaluation, although here there is a particular accent on encouraging self-criticism by grant applicants and recipients: 'Self-evaluation is the ideal – since this is less threatening than outside monitoring and more likely to continue and to have any conclusions implemented.'

The work on the Irish Republic is one aspect of a general concern with grant-making in geographical areas which, despite severe deprivation, rarely receive as much funding as South East England. Grants to the London area now account for only about seven per cent of the grant total for the Foundation, and it is liaising with the Baring Foundation to develop its work in the North East and North West of England.

THE JOSEPH ROWNTREE MEMORIAL TRUST

1. History and Background

'The soup kitchen in York never has difficulty in obtaining adequate financial aid, but an enquiry into the extent and causes of poverty would enlist little support.' It was partly to remedy this lack of support that Joseph Rowntree set up the three trusts in 1904 that now bear his name. The Charitable Trust, founded to undertake charitable works, is presently concerned mainly with peace and international relations, social justice, citizens' rights, and racial discrimination. The Social Service Trust is not a registered charity because it supports political and pressure group work which is not defined as charitable under English law. It was the Village Trust, originally established to benefit the cocoa workers' community of New Earswick near York, which had its objects widened by a private Act of Parliament in 1959 to become the Joseph Rowntree Memorial Trust. The Memorial Trust still retains its former responsibilities, but now runs a £5 million a year programme of social research and development. Following its hostile takeover in 1988, the Rowntree confectionary company (primary source of Joseph Rowntree's, and the Trusts', wealth) is no longer the principal location for the Memorial Trust's investments, but the Trust's income has benefited considerably from their sale.

The Trust broadly takes its remit from Joseph Rowntree's intention 'to seek out the underlying causes of weakness or evil', even if his noble hope, that such an enquiry would 'in the course of a few years, change the face of England', seems in retrospect to ignore the fact that many people still prefer to see the soup kitchens.

2. Objects and Policy

Research in the following areas is supported:

Housing, including homelessness, housing finance, and management of rented housing;

Social and community care, with a particular focus on the elderly, carers, and those leaving institutions;

Changes in **social security** provision;

Factors affecting those with **disabilities,** particularly mental handicap;

Improvement of **central/local government relations.**

The Trust also manages a housing association for New Earswick and other developments in the York area, and administers £8m worth of government grants each year for the families of severely disabled children through the **Family Fund.**

3. Grant Guidelines

'If it does not make a difference, it was not worth doing.' It is research directed towards improvements in practice that the Trust favours, or as Robin Guthrie, a former Director, said of an earlier policy: 'It is fairly easy to have an intelligent conversation about this, but much more difficult to think about what one might constructively do.' One of the Trust's main concerns, consequently, is the dissemination of research findings, ultimately with a view to influencing social policy. The latest Triennial Report describes the process as 'Insemination....the active introduction of ideas, knowledge and practice into existing systems'.

The Trust usually works through, or in association with, other institutions, many of them academic. It will also joint-fund projects in collaboration with other trusts, supporting for example the research side of an action research project. It is, however, unusual among grant-making trusts in taking an active, sometimes formative role in the projects that it supports: large projects might have an advisory group and many are helped to publicize their results. Of note is the Trust's symbiotic relationship with the Policy Studies Institute: it owns PSI's premises in London and supports several of its projects, in turn benefiting from the Institute's professional expertise in research.

Generally speaking, grants are *not* made for:

    National charities or general appeals;

    Revenue costs of established housing or social care projects;

    Medical research, the arts, conservation, job creation or travel;

    Educational bursaries or individual research;

    Projects whose statutory funding has been withdrawn;

    The cost of buildings or equipment;

    Conferences, seminars or publications (unless they are linked with research the Trust is supporting).

4. Trustees

Trustees' meetings take place four times a year and are chaired by Sir Donald Barron, a former Chairman of Midland Bank PLC, with Sir Charles Carter (Chair of PSI's Research Committee) as Vice-Chair. The other trustees are:

Peter Barclay CBE	William Sessions
The Rt Hon Sir Patrick Nairne GCB MC	Cedric Shaw
Nigel Naish	Erica Vere

Joseph Rowntree was a Quaker and new trustees of the Memorial Trust are now appointed alternately by the Religious Society of Friends (Quakers) and by the other trustees.

5. Staff

The Trust's Director is Richard Best OBE, whose last post was as Director of the National Federation of Housing Associations. The senior staff are:

    Eleanor Barnes, Director of Family Fund;

    Cedric Dennis, Director of Housing;

    Dr Janet Lewis, Director of Research;

    Michael Sturge, Director of Finance.

6. Grant procedure and advice to applicants

Research proposals need to be detailed and carefully planned; they are also unlikely to fit a standard format. For both these reasons, the Trust issues no application form, and a concise outline of the project will suffice at first to show if it is relevant to the Trust's ongoing concerns. If so, a full proposal will be requested on consultation with Trust staff; if not, the proposal will be rejected subject to confirmation at the next trustees' meeting (the fate of the majority). In either case, the trustees will have seen a note of the application.

In considering promising applications the trustees benefit from several aids to decision-making: the advice of the Director or member of staff who dealt with the application; the recommendations of the Housing Research Committee or the Social Research Committee which each meet between trustees' meetings to consider proposals in their area of interest; the recommendations of advisory groups to particular programmes (e.g. the Advisory Group on Disability); and, on occasion, the view of an independent expert consulted in confidence.

7. Issues

The Memorial Trust maintains that 'clear thinking based on sound evidence will indeed contribute to the solution of social problems', but it often seems rather anxious to secure the passage betwixt cup and lip, either from professional unsteadiness or a political nudge. Rather than simply floating new concepts in the social sciences, there is an emphasis on the controlled and monitored development of professional practice; this might involve the use of training programmes to implement changes in practice, which will then be evaluated using criteria derived from the original research. The Trust's current work on central/local government relations, on the other hand, could be a response to the shelving (for political reasons) of its 1986 Working Party recommendation for a standing commission on relations between central and local government.

One of the major concerns of the Trust for some time has been the role of the voluntary sector during a period of significant change, not to say hardship, for the Welfare State. Robin Guthrie wrote in the early eighties: 'There is a role for trusts to stimulate change in voluntary organisations in response to the changed circumstances that now exist....to assist organisations through a period of transition'. Richard Best, Guthrie's successor, takes up the strain: 'Good research could be timely and important in discovering whether the voluntary sector can become a major provider and whether (or how) the community can be centrally involved.' The Trust has evidenced its concern more concretely by funding research into housing co-operatives and tenant participation and by backing the Wolfenden Inquiry into the future role of the voluntary sector. Best, notably, draws a distinction between who *pays*, and who *provides*. Regarding service provision, therefore, he can talk of 'a radical shift of emphasis from the State to the voluntary sector', but, due to the level of resources involved, emphasizes at the same time that 'only public investment can cope'.

THE LORD ASHDOWN CHARITABLE TRUST

1. History and Background

The Trust was founded in 1968 by the late Lord Ashdown, formerly Sir Arnold Silverstone. It was endowed in the early seventies, and assets from Lord Ashdown's companies and his executors have built up to a fund of over £11.5 million. The current trustees are all original trustees appointed by Lord Ashdown himself.

In 1988/89 over £1 million was given in grants.

2. Objects and Policy

The objects of the Trust are listed as 'general charitable purposes'. In practice grants are made to a range of social and medical welfare charities.

3. Grant guidelines

Overall the Trust favours organisations which are unlikely to gain funding from other sources. This has meant funding for a wide spread of community-based groups which include a number of organisations working with the elderly, people who are disabled, and women's refuges. The trustees are particularly interested in prevention of illness and promotion of health. A proportion of the grants each year are earmarked for mature students, particularly medical students who are unable to find funding elsewhere. There also remains a loyalty to some of the Jewish causes favoured by Lord Ashdown himself. In fact, many of the larger grants in recent years have gone to Jewish welfare charities. A few individuals in need are helped, but usually the grants are channelled through organisations such as the Family Welfare Association.

Where salaries are involved, the Trust will try to commit three years' funding to allow for job security. This means that a substantial part of the Trust's resources are already committed from year to year.

As a general rule, grants are not made to large national charities or for:

The arts;

Expeditions or study abroad;

Private school fees or law students' fees;

Elective period costs or interconnected BSC courses of medical students;

Research of a purely academic nature.

4. Trustees

The trustees are: Clive Marks FCA, George Renwick, Dr Richard Stone, and Jonathan Silver. Aside from the Annual General Meeting, a grant-giving sub-committee meets every two to three weeks to consider applications.

5. Staff

The correspondent for the Trust is Mr Clive Marks, one of the trustees, and, as with many medium and smaller-sized trusts, other administration is handled by a firm of accountants.

6. Grant procedures and advice to applicants

Written applications should be sent to the correspondent, preferably consisting of concise details of the project, typed on one A4 sheet. Other supporting information should be attached, in particular a one-page budget showing anticipated income and expenditure for the years for which finance is being asked. The Trust also requests that any Annual Reports and Accounts should be sent with the application, and even, where relevant, photographs of activities. Unsuccessful applications will only be acknowledged if a stamped, addressed envelope is supplied.

THE LORD ASHDOWN CHARITABLE TRUST

The trustees like to meet some applicants personally; all the mature students supported, for example, are interviewed first. Projects that are funded over a longer period are required to submit an annual report to the Trust.

7. Issues

The Trust's central concern at present is one shared by many grant-making trusts: the increasing pressure to take over funding when Local or Central Government have pulled out. Richard Stone, one of the trustees, outlines the problem for grant-makers in general: 'We need to steer a tricky course between not refusing to fill the vacuum, but still not propping up policies which are damaging to worthy causes'. Possible guidelines he suggests for trusts include the practice of offering a proportion of the funding required so that this can be presented to statutory authorities or other grant-making trusts for matching funds. Additionally, 'trustees may choose to 'underwrite' the full funding in a separate communication, verbal or in a separate letter. Applicants may be offered the suggestion that 'if you do manage to find the remainder of the funds from other sources we can then divert our money to others in need''.

The Lord Ashdown Trust in particular will often give applicants help and advice in pressing statutory funders before making a decision on giving its own grant. This, however, can only mitigate the frustration trustees feel now 'that they are becoming the ultimate arbiters of whether a voluntary organisation is going to continue or die'.

THE PADDINGTON CHARITIES

Comprising the Paddington Charitable Estates Educational Fund and the Paddington Welfare Charities

1. History and Background

Originally a diverse group of charities for the education and welfare of residents of Paddington, the Paddington Charitable Estates and Welfare Charities were partially amalgamated by successive schemes of the Charity Commissioners, the last being in 1977. Assets are now held in a General Account, four-fifths of the income going to the Educational Fund and one-fifth to the Welfare Charities. The Paddington Welfare Charities consist of the Relief in Need account and the Relief in Sickness account, of which the first has a significant endowment of its own. In 1988 the income of the Educational Fund was £80,000 and the income of the Welfare Charities about half that amount.

The Charities are now administered by Westminster City Council through a body of independent trustees chosen from the Paddington area.

2. Objects and Policy

The Educational Fund supports voluntary schools and other educational organisations in Paddington, and also assists individuals with maintenance, fees and equipment to enable them to pursue educational courses or enter a profession or trade. It will also make grants for essential clothing for school children and for educational holidays.

The Welfare Charities make grants to relieve any Paddington resident who is in need or distress, or is sick, convalescent, disabled, handicapped or infirm.

3. Grant Guidelines

The Charities point out that 'as long as the need is clear, the trustees have a wide scope in the sort of relief they can give.' The restrictions are that the money is not used to relieve public funds, that grants to pay salaries are not provided, and that the beneficiary lives in the area of the former Metropolitan Borough of Paddington, i.e. the North West part of the City of Westminster bounded by Maida Vale and Edgware Road to the East and the Bayswater Road to the South. An additional restriction for the Educational Fund only is that beneficiaries must be less than 25 years old.

The Educational Fund commits the bulk of its resources to voluntary schools, youth clubs and other organisations. Grants to individuals include a scheme to give pocket money to needy children in Paddington schools. The scheme is administered through the Inner London Education Authority, as is the Fund's grant to enable poor families to have a holiday.

The Welfare Charities generally pay for items, services or facilities to alleviate the situation of individuals in need. They also distribute food and fuel coupons, and pay pensions of £10 a month to about 80 pensioners. Small gifts are distributed by local churches at Christmas. As with the Educational Fund, some of its income reaches those in need through an allocation to other welfare organisations. An annual grant is made to the local Age Concern, and Westminster Social Services receives a block grant to make emergency grants through an Amenities Fund.

4. Trustees

The Scheme of 1961 states 'the body of Trustees shall consist when complete of nine competent persons residing or carrying on business in or near Paddington'. Among the trustees are representatives from the local churches. New trustees are appointed by the local authority.

Full trustees' meetings are held twice a year, in April and October. They are chaired by Michael Kenyon, the Chairman of Kenyon Securities, one of the largest funeral directors in the UK (now in the process of merging with two other firms).

5. Staff

The local authority officers responsible for the Charities are:

R G Brooke, Clerk to the Trustees

Helen Moss, Deputy Clerk to the Trustees

G R Packman, Accountant and Financial Adviser

Applications are normally dealt with by Helen Moss, who is also responsible for handling applications for a number of other local charities. She works as Chief Assistant in the Grants Unit of Westminster Council, which gives financial support to local voluntary organisations.

6. Grant procedure and advice to applicants

Applications should be made on behalf of individuals by social services or welfare agencies (eg. by a social worker or teacher). There is no standard form but applications should include details of the financial circumstances of the intended beneficiary, full costing of the item(s) needed, and a note of other charities applied to for the same purpose. The eligibility of a particular case can usually be clarified by a telephone call to Helen Moss.

In order that grants can be made as the need arises, applications for small grants are normally dealt with on submission, and are approved by a minimum of the Chair and one other trustee.

7. Issues

Michael Kenyon, the Chair of the trustees, notes that the number of applications received has risen recently, but doubts whether this will have much effect on how the Charities operate, preferring to see their work as a continuum: 'The Charities have been extremely active over the years, and I see no reason why that should change'. In fact the Paddington Charities demonstrate a curious mixture of charitable practices, both old and new. The distribution of Christmas boxes through the local parish church is perhaps a rather Victorian image of charity, but the Charities are also notable for working with professional educational and welfare agencies (both voluntary and statutory), thus giving their grant-making a degree of efficiency and comprehensiveness that probably would not be possible if they had to rely on their own limited resources.

The Charities also display considerable success in targeting grants to the grey areas where urgent need exists but which strictly fall outside the responsibility of statutory bodies. They might indeed have had a small effect in stretching the area of statutory responsibility, for example, by making some of their grants conditional on corresponding spending by ILEA. Many of the grants, then, whether for higher education, household equipment, or general welfare, are made to individuals who miss qualifying for a statutory grant or benefit. In the words of Michael Kenyon: 'If people fall through the net, then we look after it'.

THE OTHER TRUST

1. History and Background

Originally attached to a home for orphans and unmarried mothers with children, the Trust had its objects widened when the Home was closed down. The sale fifteen years ago of some land the Trust had acquired on the outskirts of London at the turn of the century has made it quite rich. It now has an income of about £150,000 a year.

2. Objects

General charitable purposes.

3. Trustees and Staff

There are six trustees, of whom five are male, middle-aged, middle-class and white. The other is female, middle-aged, middle-class and white. Like most trusts, new trustees are appointed by the present incumbents. Family connection is the principal criterion for selection. The Trust employs one person to provide part-time secretarial assistance.

Trustees meet once a year, to consider applications and to approve grants. They work from just the original copy of the application, to keep photocopying costs down.

4. Grant Procedure

Chairman: Well, as most of us are here, I suggest we get going and hopefully Mrs Harold will turn up soon. Shall we begin with the application for sixty thousand pounds from Bamford Care for Children? As you all know, we've been supporting Bamford Care for Children for a number of years now, for their excellent work in the community, with the children, and their families, providing a much-needed service, and this grant would enable them to continue that work, giving a helping-hand to children who really don't get very much else. I'm sure I don't need to stress to you that....

2nd Trustee: Yes, I think we're all agreed here, yes?

All: Agreed.

Chairman: Well, in my capacity as Chairman of Bamford Care for Children, I would like to express our gratitude to the trustees for the interest, and the generosity, they have shown, and I can assure them that the money has found a very worthy cause, and that it will be used to benefit a great many children. And I know that if those children could meet you themselves, they would....

Secretary: Er, yes, Charles, thank you. Shall we, er, shall we move on?

Chairman: Of course, of course.

Secretary: The Housing Advice Line have put in an application for an action research project on homelessness. They propose to set up a temporary accomodation hot line, and then monitor the flow of residents through a number of selected hostels. They're asking for twenty thousand in all, and they've costed it out in some detail. That includes installing the lines and the switchboard, one part-time worker with volunteer help, some publicity, data collection....They think they can get a Polytechnic lecturer to produce the report on just out-of-pocket expenses.

2nd Trustee: I don't see the point of the research bit. I mean we all know that these people are homeless, don't we?

Secretary: What do you think, Charles?

4th Trustee: Excuse me, could I see the application?

Secretary: Yes, in just a minute. Charles?

Chairman: It does seem a lot of money. We are quite a small trust and I don't know if we can commit ourselves to too many projects of this size. Paul, what's your opinion?

145

THE OTHER TRUST

4th Trustee: Excuse....

5th Trustee: I'm with you on this one, Charles. It's the size of the grant that makes you hesitate. After all, there's never any guarantee that it will be well spent in the end.

4th Trustee: The application....please?

Secretary: Oh, I'm sorry. Here you are. Well, we seem to be agreed. I'll write and tell them it's outside our scope. Did you want to say something, Stephen?

4th Trustee: Er....er....well....no.

Secretary: Next, there's an application from Billinghampton Pony Club for the cost of some extra equipment and a new pony. They're going to provide riding lessons on Saturday mornings for the children from the nearby hospital for the mentally-handicapped. Although, I must admit, I don't really see why they need the new stuff just to do that....

2nd Trustee: Yes, they're wasting our time basically.

4th Trustee: Could I have a look?

Secretary: I don't think it's worth your trouble, Stephen. It isn't even very well presented.

Chairman: Yes, let's press on.

Secretary: Right then, an application for initial funding for a community support project for juvenile offenders in Welsdon. The project will be run from....

(Mrs Harold arrives)

Mrs Harold: I am sorry. I'm so dreadfully late. Has my pony club come up yet?

Secretary: Er....

4th Trustee: Er....

5th Trustee: Er....

Chairman: Er....yes, we gave it five thousand pounds.

Mrs Harold: Oh good.

Chairman (aside to Sec): Get that down.

Secretary: We were....we were just discussing initial funding for the Welsdon juvenile offenders community support project. The project

146

is going to be run from the local community centre at....

Mrs Harold: Do you think we ought to be giving money away to criminals?

Secretary: Well, it's....it's not quite like that. Most of the young people are first-time offenders, and are having some difficulty in readjusting to....

2nd Trustee: They should have thought of that before.

Secretary: ....in readjusting to a normal life within the community, and....

Chairman: Yes, I don't really think it's our cup of tea. We don't have very much money and we don't need to get involved in that....in that sort of thing. Next.

Secretary: Next, Action for the Aged down in Broughton want four thousand for a home-visiting scheme. It will involve volunteers going....

5th Trustee: Doesn't old Ticknell's daughter do that sort of thing? What's her name....Maggie....Margie....

Chairman: Maureen.

5th Trustee: Ah, yes. Maureen.

Chairman: Yes, that's right. Goes off after school she does.

5th Trustee: Well, it sounds a very good project indeed. Just the sort of thing we should be supporting.

2nd Trustee: By the way, are we going to invite old Ticknell to the Trust Dinner this year?

Mrs Harold: Yes, the Trust Dinner, where shall we have it this year? I thought the Brooks's Club last year was a bit stuffy. What about 'La Maison des Herbes' in Lingham Road?

Chairman: I'm not so sure. I thought their foie gras wasn't quite up to it. Anyway it's rather expensive, and small, and if we held it there we'd have to make it only trustees and their wives. Oh – I'm sorry, and husbands.

Secretary: Yes, we are trying....er....trying to keep Trust administration costs down this year....

THE OTHER TRUST

This, of course, is entirely fictitious. But it does have a ring of truth. Many trusts and most of the smaller trusts do not have formal guidelines or employ professional staff. The trustees meet infrequently. They are often drawn from a tightly-knit circle. They may give preference to their own projects or to activities which are known to them personally. The principal object of the meeting may be to get through the business as quickly as possible. The discussion may be ill-informed or irrational. The trustees may not even have been properly briefed. Not all trusts operate this way, but this is the background against which some of the trusts you are approaching will be considering your application and deciding whether to offer you a grant.

This and the real case studies that preceded it were written by Mark Lattimer.

Trust Monitor
& Grant News

A comprehensive information service for all those raising money from trusts, containing:

> The latest facts and figures on grant-making by major trusts.
>
> Details of new and newly-identified larger trusts.
>
> Updates on changes in trust policy, administration and addresses.
>
> Profiles of trust administrators.
>
> Articles and features of matter of current interest and concern.

Available on subscription only three times a year, in May, October and February each year.

Published by the Directory of Social Change, an annual subsciption costs £20, post-free. Available from the Directory of Social Change, Radius Works, Back Lane, London NW3 1HL.

A Guide to the Major Trusts

Edited by Luke FitzHerbert and Michael Eastwood.

This guide provides more detail than has ever been published before on the grant-making policies and practices of major charitable trusts. Besides providing general information on each trust's background, interests and priorities, their grant-making is illustrated with details of actual grants made in the latest year, for which information is available.

It covers over 400 grant-making trusts and foundations which together make grants of about £250 million to charity each year, plus 40 further charities which make grants for medical research.

Paperback, £12.50
Hardback, £25

Published by the Directory of Social Change, and available post-free from the Directory of Social Change, Radius Works, Back Lane, London NW3 1HL.

The Directory of Social Change

The Directory of Social Change is an educational charity which was set up in 1975. It serves as the leading publisher of grant guides and advisory handbooks for the voluntary sector. Publications concentrate on aspects of fund-raising and financial management for charities and voluntary organisations. The Directory also runs a range of training courses, seminars and conferences covering the same field of interest. Finally, it acts as an innovator in introducing new projects and approaches to charities.

For further information and an up-to-date booklist or courses brochure, write to:

The Directory of Social Change,
Radius Works,
Back Lane,
London
NW3 1HL

01-435 8171
01-431 1817